BLIND ACCEPTANCE

BLIND ACCEPTANCE

SANDRA PIMENTEL

Author's Note: I have tried to recreate events, locales, and conversations from my memories of them. In order to maintain their anonymity, in some instances I have changed the names of individuals and places. I may have changed some identifying characteristics and details such as physical properties, occupations, and places of residence.

Print information available on the last page.

AUTHOR PHOTO CREDIT:

Adventure Photo   customerservicephoto@vallarta-adventures.com

Rev. date: 08/23/2016

CONTENTS

Acknowledgements.. xi

INTRODUCTION

Quincy, Massachusetts xv

PART 1

Chapter One: Sabatino and his Son Panfilio 1
Chapter Two: Pamp and Dorothy Meet 6
Chapter Three: My Mother's Line... 9
Chapter Four: Richard 13
Chapter Five: Life in Braintree 15
Chapter Six: At Mah and Pah's 21
Chapter Seven: About Mom and Dad 26
Chapter Eight: Grandma Bessie 29
Chapter Nine: Pah Dies 33
Chapter Ten: Another Death... 37
Chapter Eleven: Childhood Challenges................................. 39
Chapter Twelve: Growing Up Easy, "Feeling Life Hard" 42
Chapter Thirteen: Nursing School Friends............................ 45
Chapter Fourteen: Intervention 49
Chapter Fifteen: Propose and Compromise 51
Chapter Sixteen: Marriage.. 64
Chapter Seventeen: Motherhood 70
Chapter Eighteen: Dickie 78
Chapter Nineteen: At Last 85

PART 2

Chapter Twenty: Family and Community Life...................... 89
Chapter Twenty-One: Alignment... 104

PART 3

Chapter Twenty-Two: Blind Acceptance and Stark Reality... 123
Chapter Twenty-Three: Nightmare 137
Chapter Twenty-Four: Withdrawal 140
Chapter Twenty-Five: Risks and Warnings.......................... 144
Chapter Twenty-Six: More Surprises 147
Chapter Twenty-Seven: Distraction....................................157
Chapter Twenty-Eight: The Beginning of the End 160

PART 4

Chapter Twenty-Nine: The Medical Entertainments Begin...181
Chapter Thirty: Back To New England 187
Chapter Thirty-One: Paul-Otics 190
Chapter Thirty-Two: Moving On – Again 199
Chapter Thirty-Three: The Blizzard of '78........................... 203
Chapter Thirty-Four: Midlife Crisis..................................... 206
Chapter Thirty-Five: Solar Panels and Sitting Bull.............. 209
Chapter Thirty-Six: My Turn...213
Chapter Thirty-Seven: Our Children 215
Chapter Thirty-Eight: Pequod...217
Chapter Thirty-Nine: Our Italian Daughter 220
Chapter Forty: Therein Lies Happiness 222
Chapter Forty-One: Berkley Circle Turnaround................... 224
Chapter Forty-Two: Old Horizons Made New 226
Chapter Forty-Three: Reconciliation 231

PART 5

Chapter Forty-Four: A Dream Comes True 237
Chapter Forty-Five: Work 238
Chapter Forty-Six: Bridges to Islam 240
Chapter Forty-Seven: Berkley Circle Sale 243
Chapter Forty-Eight: Full Circle 249
Chapter Forty-Nine: Let the Construction Begin 252
Chapter Fifty: The Net Result 254
Chapter Fifty-One: The Legacy Goes On 255
Chapter Fifty-Two: 50th Wedding Anniversary 259
Chapter Fifty-Three: A Circle of Acceptance 262

Combined Family Tree 266
Pasquale Family Tree 267
Leet Family Tree 268

APPENDIX: IN CELEBRATION OF MY FAMILY

Chapter One: My Ancestors 271
Chapter Two: Paternal Ancestors 273
Chapter Three: Maternal Ancestors 283
Chapter Four: The Generation Before Me 285
Chapter Five: Maternal Aunts and Uncles 289
Chapter Six: Paternal Aunts – The Pasquale Women 291
Chapter Seven: Paternal Uncles – The Pasquale Men 298

Dedicated to my husband Paul,
the source of my peace

ACKNOWLEDGEMENTS

Thank you to my:

- brilliant husband Paul Pimentel, who supports me every single day,
- mother Dorothy, who told me I should write this book,
- father Panfilio, who was my inspiration and role model,
- grandfather Sabatino, who quietly set a standard of caring, trust, and generosity,
- editor and friend Susan Klein, who used her amazing skills to help me write in straight lines,
- Cousin Dolores, who validated my memories, and knew the answers,
- friends, the Goldbergs, Dands, and Langs, who've shared the best and worst of times, and

especially to Jerry Goldberg, the brother of my heart, and the kindest man I know.

Thank you generation six—my children:

Lisa, Christopher, Susan, Joanie, and Courtney, in particular Lisa—your encouragement through hours of tearful writing and your keen eye have been invaluable—and Joanie—your willingness to teach your old mother new technical tricks was not an easy feat.

Thank you to my friends: Anthony and Eileen DiBenedetto, Mache Seibel, Barbara and Tom Gladney, Ron and Bonnie Dunlap, Cliff and Judy Genge, Joan Kriegstein, Susie Wasserman, Rose Styron, Kati Delahunt, Paul and Joanne Guzzi, Elaine Miller, Lois Rudnick, Jewelle Gibbs, Margo Long, John Kennedy, Julie Fay, Arnie Reisman, and Mary Ann and Stanley Snider for being there when I needed you. Your consistent encouragement matters to me.

Thanks to my friend Bill Delahunt for giving me the time to grow up; and to Bill Keating for trusting me when I was grown.

Thank you to my young friend Julius for the gift of the cover painting.

I am thankful for my ancestors who set the stage for a life of blind acceptance.

INTRODUCTION

QUINCY, MASSACHUSETTS

I was born in 1942 at the Harley Hospital in Boston. My mother said it was a terrible birth because her doctor, an old Italian man, believed women should suffer. My father told me that when I finally arrived, I looked like a squirrel. My parents both said that it wasn't until my hair fell out that I was beautiful.

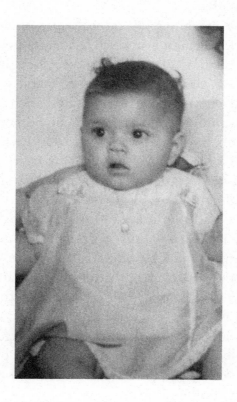

Sandra Pasquale at one year old

In my early years we lived on Edinboro Road in a small section of the City of Quincy Massachusetts called the Point. The two story-houses on both sides of our street stood *square* and closely together on barren lots with unkempt grass and a few random hollyhocks held tightly to the dry earth. In some ways it felt like an early version of a housing project reflecting the muted tone of The Great Depression and World War II about to end.

When I was a very little girl I loved the weekends. On Fridays, Daddy got paid, so he'd often bring home a surprise. My favorite was a doll that could turn from sad to happy in a flash, and I slept with her every night.

On Saturday mornings my father and I often had parades. We'd go to the kitchen and each select a large spoon and worthy pot to serve as a drum. My Dad would then begin to sing out a John Philip Sousa march as loudly as he could without using a single word, and we banged on our pots in tandem as we marched with great gusto around our tiny apartment. Sometimes he would forgo the utensils and use the palm-under-the-armpit trick to simulate the brass section. My mother was never amused as my father looked at her impishly. I, on the other hand, would giggle and laugh until I could stand it no more.

Although we had few luxuries on Edinboro Road, life was enriched by my relatives—aunts, uncles, and cousins from both sides of my family—and by our neighbors who were Italians, Scots, Irish, and Jews, evidence of the immigration surge that transformed America around the turn of the century.

As we children ran around our neighborhood on warm days, the scent of tomato sauce and the sound of sausages crackling on iron skillets spilled from open windows. Everyone took care of and disciplined all the children so we all suffered the scrutiny of every adult in the neighborhood.

Children gathered on a summer's day in the Point: FRONT:
Far right: Sandra sitting next to Cousin Dolores; BACK:
Uncle Rudy (Rudolpho) behind and between the girls

In the midst of it all, a subtle sadness surrounded me in those very early years, but I had no idea then of its origins. I now wonder if it was related to the melancholy that permeates the aftermath of troubled times as I frequently heard stories about what it was like to live with food shortages and through the sacrifices of war.

Though I was only three when World War II ended, I recall the day with remarkable clarity. My parents sat on the sofa in our sparse living room listening to the mahogany radio that was as tall as I. When the news poured through the fabric of the speaker, my parents' faces registered relief rather than joy. I had no idea what war was or what had happened, but I understood it was the end of something really horrible.

When my parents had absorbed the weight of the news, my father and I left our second floor apartment and went down to the street where many people had gathered in jubilation. The children clanged pots and pans as we all marched up one street and down the other.

In my childhood days there were few toys; my imagination and the visual images that the radio evoked replaced them. My favorite pastime as a little girl in the 1940s was listening to "The Lone Ranger" on the radio. I always fantasized that I would marry him one day.

In the Point we all lived simply while perched on the edge of poverty, but there was always mutual support and my Italian relatives had a unique ability to create joyful times and to eat well in the midst of it all.

Radio was the primary entertainment in those days but my Pasquale and Faiella families turned the gossip of the day into compelling drama. Theatrics were evident every day in the Point. Discussing stories about relatives who were absent was a sport that they all loved and they would play "Ain't it Awful" for hours on end. Their mantra of, "You don't know what I've *been* through!" reflected their one-upmanship of misery—such a *happy* family—and all so *miserable.*

While gossip was my family's primary sport, they would never tolerate someone outside the family indulging in chatter about our family's business. *"Don't tell anybody, but . . ."* was another common introduction. While keeping a secret within the family was nearly impossible, the news rarely traveled beyond the circle of our relatives, because *family loyalty* is *family loyalty.*

PART 1

CHAPTER ONE

Sabatino and his Son Panfilio

When my father was born in 1918, Italians were considered *less than,* and with his nose and a name like Panfilio Pasquale, his cultural heritage was never in doubt. Though he was baptized Panfilo, somehow he became Panfilio (pron. Pan feel` ee-o). The reason for the change remains a mystery, but Daddy always said his name was a blessing. "With a name like mine, I had to be strong," he'd say. Maybe it was for cultural balance but more likely just for fun that he took the name Henry at his confirmation.

Manny Arruda (possibly) and Panfilio on the old truck

Eventually Panfilio Henry Pasquale became "Pamp."

He was born to Emma (née) Faiella and Sabatino (later known as Sam) Pasquale on June 11, 1918 and was the first son after the birth of his four sisters—Philomena (Philly), Maria (Mary,) Egla (Cookie,) and Irma (Betty); he was born before his five brothers Ulysses (Willie), Mario, Luigi (Punky), Aristide (Eddie), and finally Rudolpho (Rudy, whom his brothers often called Pouffa.) While many of these names were common to Italian immigrants, they all had been changed to American nicknames to fit their multi-cultural neighborhood and xenophobic society.

SEATED: Eddie, Willy, Punky, and Mario;
STANDING: Cookie, Pamp, and Betty

As the oldest boy, Pamp enjoyed a kind of exalted status; his brothers looked up to him and his sisters indulged his every whim. He had an inordinate amount of self-confidence—enough to believe he was extraordinary. Emerging from that secure place, he couldn't and wouldn't tolerate ethnic insults. The truth is—he *was* extraordinary.

Pamp was a young teen when his father Sabatino purchased the family home on Edwards Street in the Point. It was by *barely implicit* cultural design that the children would remain in the house or neighborhood with their parents (and/or Italian spouses) forever.

By 1937 the Pasquale family had endured the Great Depression for almost eight years. Sabatino's construction company had held up well enough to provide him a living to support his family. In addition he grew vegetables and raised chickens and rabbits to help keep his family well fed. His hard work allowed him to help Emma's siblings as well. Sabatino was the kind of man who quietly carried the world on his shoulders without complaint.

This *was* my grandfather.

Pamp was very social and he had many friendships that went beyond his family. In spite of a life saturated in Italian culture, he always embraced others. He was funny, demonstrative, sometimes volatile, and always "on stage." People connected with him instantly—and more importantly—they trusted him.

When Pamp was growing up, at the invitation of his Jewish neighbors, he served as Shabbas goy[1] at the synagogue down the street on Friday nights. He always talked about his job there with pride and took comfort in knowing that his Jewish neighbors didn't care that he was an Italian. In many ways they had much in common.

---

1   a non-Jew employed by Orthodox Jews to perform services (such as turning lights on and off) which are forbidden to Jews on the Sabbath (Merriam Webster Dictionary)

When my father quit high school in his senior year to take a job in the nearby shipyard, Sabatino was furious. He'd been a good student and his father wanted more for his son. But Pamp couldn't see how staying in school would make a difference to his future. It was a steady job, after all, and the family could use the income. Pamp had tried to sign up for the military, but they wouldn't take him because of his flat feet.

It always bothered him that he didn't serve, but he was happy that he could build ships for the war effort, and there were many of them built in the forties in a short amount of time.

As a teen he was already concerned about people. Exiting a local downtown market on a bitter cold night, Pamp spotted a man with no coat standing on the corner. The fair-skinned stranger was blue, shivering, and clearly in trouble. So Pamp gave him his coat and gestured for the man to follow him home.

When they arrived at the house, it was dark and quiet. Pamp and his new acquaintance quietly walked by his parents' room and crept ever so slowly up the stairs.

When they reached the bedroom, his five brothers were sleeping in three large beds; Pamp instructed the man to crawl into bed with Mario and Punky, so the stranger slipped gently under the covers, disturbing neither. Pamp joined Rudy and there was barely a stir as all seven seemingly slept through the night.

It was still dark in the morning when Pamp left for his job in the shipyard, leaving the other six asleep.

When Emma yelled up the stairs for her sons to come down to breakfast, they trickled down the steps sporadically, the stranger following them into the kitchen. He moved toward an empty seat at the table and sat down confidently.

At first Sam and Emma ignored him. Cousins often stayed the night and extras were hardly noticed. But something about this man was different. That he was blond they could see, but when they realized he didn't speak English or Italian, they began to wonder. Emma stood behind the stranger as she shrugged her shoulders in question, and two of Pamp's brothers discretely shrugged back, indicating that they, too, had no clue.

Emma could speak Roman Italian with perfection because of her privileged upbringing, but English always remained a challenge for her. So, she addressed the stranger with, "Scuzzi, tu e famiglia?" ("Are you family?")

In response, the man quickly shrugged his shoulders indicating that he didn't understand, and went on eating his breakfast.

In the end, the man got up from the table and left the house wearing the coat Pamp had given him the night before. As the brothers hopped into the back of their father's open truck, the man walked off down the street and was never seen again.

At the dinner table that night Pamp talked about the poor guy from Finland who stood in downtown Quincy Square with no coat. Mario, who was six-foot-five, responded, "Yeah, he kicked my ribs all night and hogged the bed. I thought it was Cousin Louie."

This story *is* my father.

CHAPTER TWO

Pamp and Dorothy Meet

Pamp had tried to woo a girl named Dorothy Leet at dance clubs where they both enjoyed the swing music, but she wasn't sure about his intentions. He was a great dancer and Dorothy was always impressed when he was the center of attention on the dance floor. They danced well together and she too got attention when she danced with him.

But Dorothy was by nature a prim and proper young lady who had little exposure to any culture outside of her own WASP background. She was living at home and working in a laundry to help support the family. She was an accepting person by nature, but Pamp was different from any other young man she had known and her father had warned her to stay away from Italians. In spite of this she found Pamp to be suave and compelling.

Now Pamp's sisters were among his biggest fans and allies. Betty was a flamboyant character who made friends easily and she had become friends with Dorothy. Because Betty had a plan, she didn't let on that she was Pamp's sister.

Betty was dating Olindy, a wealthy, older businessman from Italy (whom she later married), and she asked Dorothy if she would consider going out to dinner with her, Olindy, and Pamp— on a double date. Dorothy agreed, thinking that she would feel safe if her girl friend was with her.

When Betty began to flirt with Pamp at the dinner table, Dorothy became incensed, then increasingly jealous, and amazed that Betty's Italian boyfriend Olindy would tolerate such behavior.

Later, in the ladies room, Betty talked about how wonderful Pamp was and how lucky Dorothy was to be with him. Dorothy was clearly aggravated; Betty's plan had worked.

Several weeks later, Dorothy was walking down the street with another friend, when Betty approached from the opposite direction.

Dorothy's friend said, "Here comes Pamp's sister, Betty."

At first Dorothy was in denial. "That's *not* Pamp's *sister*." But then she realized what they had done.

Dorothy had a limited capacity for pranks. However, she wasn't angry, and in fact, was relieved that Betty *hadn't* been flirting with Pamp, because, by this time, she was in love with him. Shortly thereafter, Dorothy and Pamp went to Maine with one of his married cousins and *his* wife as witnesses so that they could get married secretly.

Sam suspected the marriage, and purposely gave Pamp many glasses of homemade wine, and thus discovered that the two had eloped. The news was not well-received by either family.

Sam shared the news of the marriage with the rest of the Pasquales. Because Dorothy was *Protestant* and also not *Italian*, some of Pamp's relatives carried on with great drama. When they came marching into the honeymoon apartment several weeks after the elopement to demand that the marriage be annulled, Pamp was furious. "Get out—get the hell out of here, *now*!"

Dorothy sat cowering and horrified. She wasn't used to loud words, or yelling of any kind. Even when her father was furious, he never raised his voice.

The dramatic Italian relatives had to be reconciled to Dorothy being the first non-Italian member of the family, and they all now knew their brother was not to be challenged. High drama was a typical reaction, but it was also in the nature of the Pasquale family to take everyone in. So, naturally, Pamp and Dorothy moved into the Pasquale house on Edwards Street with his parents and remaining siblings. Dorothy shared a room with her friend Betty and with Cookie, while Pamp slept with his brothers.

As a young bride Dorothy was full of anxiety and insecurity, and in spite of the fact that she was creative, smart, diplomatic, and strong in character, she was completely over-shadowed by the weight of Pamp's personality, and by those of his relatives.

Within months the new couple found an apartment in the Point and settled in. By then, the Pasquale family had agreed that Dorothy was wonderful.

Emma believed that it was Dorothy instead of Pamp's flat feet that kept him out of WWII, which made Dorothy more popular. This was evident in that Emma taught her daughter-in-law how to cook; Dorothy quickly learned to cook Italian dishes exceptionally well in spite of coming from a Scottish-English family that didn't understand the importance of *the sauce*.

CHAPTER THREE

My Mother's Line

Elizabeth Livingston Rodger (Bessie) and Geoffrey (pron. *Jeff* ree) Leet met and later married in Halifax, Nova Scotia. On Pine Street in Dartmouth, Nova Scotia, Dorothy Elizabeth Leet (who would one day become my mother) was born on February 14, 1921. The birth took place in her paternal grandfather's house in the same room where her father Geoffrey had been born. She was christened at Christ Episcopal Church in Dartmouth.

Grandmother Elizabeth Livingston and Geoffrey Leet

Bessie gave birth to Margaret (Peggy) in Canada in 1924. Dorothy and Peggy lived with separate relatives for a time while Geoffrey sought work as a skilled electrician in the United States that same year. Such separations were frequent because of poverty and the lack of employment.

The children stayed in Canada and Bessie joined Geoffrey in the States. In 1930 the family reunited and lived in Braintree, Massachusetts. By this time there were three girls—Dorothy, Peggy, and Barbara.

Geoffrey was a harsh disciplinarian, but Dorothy managed to escape her father's wrath by not challenging him. Barbara and Peggy were more resistant and were whipped with a leather strap for their defiance. Dorothy could do nothing to stop it and reported that she felt helpless and upset at her inability to protect her sisters.

Geoffrey worked in the shipyard in Quincy. Within a few years, he contracted rheumatic fever which damaged his heart. He was seldom able to work during the Great Depression or thereafter.

As sick as Geoffrey was, he must have had periods of relative health, because after Bessie had their fourth daughter Eva, they had two more children—a girl Mary and a son Geoffrey (pronounced *Joff* ree).

FRONT: Barbara, Mary, Geoffrey; BACK:
Peggy (Margaret) and Dorothy

Geoffrey's illness left his family with few options. When Bessie went to work to support the family, Dorothy, as the oldest, was left to care for her siblings. After she graduated from high school, she went to work to help her mother pay for food and the mortgage.

It was during that time that she met Pamp and eventually married him. Geoffrey was a stubborn, serious, and narrow-minded man, the antithesis of the spontaneous and fun-loving Italians in Pamp's family (who might rant and rave one day, and dismiss such drama the next). Of the three daughters, Dorothy was the most compliant. Yet, she had married an Italian and Geoffrey was incensed. Unlike Pamp's family, he did *not* yell and scream one day and forget it the *next*. Rather, he sulked and refused to see Dorothy—ever again!

While her husband would *not* change his mind, Bessie, who was more easy-going, didn't share his opinion and embraced her daughter's decision. Nonetheless, Geoffrey was galvanized in his rejection of Dorothy and her new husband.

Bessie started visiting Dorothy and Pamp sometime after they got married. Geoffrey still refused. When I was born in 1942, my grandfather Geoffrey refused to see *me* as well. Even so, he would drive Grandma Bessie to our house, and then wait in the car outside of our apartment while she visited us. It's impressive that my grandmother was brave enough to go against Geoffrey's wishes, not likely something she did easily.

It took her a very long while, but finally, my mother mustered up enough courage and anger to go to the car to confront her father. "You have a beautiful granddaughter, and you've already missed so much of her life. When will you stop this?" My grandfather saw me for the first time when I was two years old.

He died on May 31, 1946. I barely knew him but remember that he played the fiddle and was quiet. I don't recall him expressing any emotions or affection toward me or anyone else for that matter. I saw him on his deathbed in the living room on Holden Road in Braintree, Massachusetts, where he lived with my grandmother, Aunt Mary, and Uncle Geoffrey (Joff), who were only teenagers then.

My father was at Grandpa Geoffrey's bedside when he took his last breath at forty-two years of age. I was four and my mother was pregnant. Ironically, my grandfather had taken to my father and wanted Pamp next to him when he passed. Perhaps in the end, he saw the narrow-mindedness of his bigotry, or maybe my father had succeeded in captivating him with his charm.

CHAPTER FOUR

Richard

Born in 1946, my little brother was named Richard Panfilio Pasquale—a big name for a tiny baby. My mother was reluctant to give such an unusual name to her newborn, but my father felt he'd learned to be confident and independent because of his name, and he wanted his son to have the same advantage.

On the day my brother Dickie was born, I waited on the steps of Grandma Bessie's house as the entourage followed him into the house. My mother carried my infant brother with extreme care and I could see that her usual level of anxiety had reached an all-time high. As they all walked by, my mother said, "Wait here until the baby gets changed." I barely got a glimpse of his little round face.

My brother's birth changed my world, but I never really minded. I loved Dickie who grew to be much more attached to my mother than I was. It was a relief to have my mother worry about him rather than me.

Dickie was an adorable little boy, and when he was three and I was seven we were inseparable.

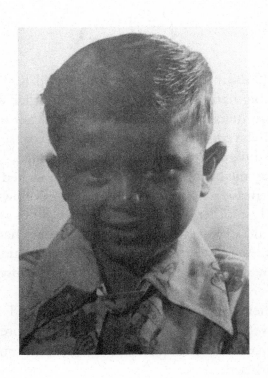

Dickie at 3 years

Chapter Five

Life in Braintree

We moved from The Point into my maternal grandmother Bessie's house on Holden Road when I was eight years old and Dickie four.

Living together was a good thing for Grandma Bessie. Since my grandfather Geoffrey had died several years earlier, she'd struggled to hold onto the house. My parents took over all house expenses, including the rent.

Grandma Bessie's house wasn't much bigger than our small apartment in Quincy, but even with five of us together, it felt fine. The bright and welcoming bungalow had lots of windows and a brick fireplace in the small living room. A bathroom with two doors separated two small bedrooms—my parents had one and I shared the other with my grandmother. There was a small dining room where Dickie slept on a studio couch and the kitchen had a table large enough to accommodate us all. My mother was creative enough to turn our new house into a sweet little finished cottage.

In some ways, though, Braintree was like a different country. Nonetheless, the arrangement seemed to work for all of us.

While my mother loved my father's family, the chaos and enmeshed Italian family life had been difficult for her. Another difference was that my Scottish grandmother boiled everything to mush, a far cry from the Italian feasts we were used to. But my mother seemed happy to be with her own mother in a peaceful place.

My father, on the other hand, missed his life in The Point where feelings flew all around all the time. Daddy seemed to be conspiring to go *home* for one reason or another, and it irritated my mother, who saw through his endless excuses to get to the Italian club, the Torre D' Passieri in Quincy, which he loved and where many of his friends and family hung out.

Part of me missed the freedom of expression and honesty that came with people saying whatever they wanted to say without reservation. While other families carried grudges for days, or even years, the atmosphere of my Italian grandparents' house had been like a tornado; my Italian relatives were programmed to feel emotions intensely and then to let them go. Things always calmed down and joy eventually prevailed.

In Braintree, my father became more subdued, realizing that a simple argument would devastate his mother-in-law, Bessie. He let Bessie know that he loved her company, and we all followed suit. She seemed to be truly happy when we all lived together. My father made her laugh and encouraged her to enjoy life more freely—and she did.

Elizabeth (Bessie) Leet

Sometimes I was able to spend the weekend at my godparents, Floss and Don Remick's, who had been Grandma Bessie's best friends for many years. I loved it there because I had my own bedroom that was tucked away upstairs, with a small bathroom. I also loved that their old house smelled of wood, and that I could be in my room without much interference.

My godparents never had children of their own, so I was a special addition to their lives. My brother was invited too, but he wouldn't leave my mother's side and come with me to my special place.

While my mother always let me run free in Braintree, it was much better at Auntie Floss and Uncle Don's house. I'd go to the nearby field to pick blueberries and do things I would never have been able to do if my brother and mother had been with me.

My godmother would scrub me every night, and change the sheets every day, but she let me make mud pies in a contrived pit under the spigot right up against the house. They had a barn with chickens, and a big black dog that loved me as much as they did. I had chores there that I always did with pleasure, and I loved playing in their rickety old barn. When they tore it down and built a new garage, I missed the musty smell of the old beams and being able to crawl up into the loft. I loved being with people, but I could appreciate solitude.

The Fore River Shipyard in The Point had provided many jobs in the area; both my father and grandfather Geoffrey had worked there. During World War II, Bethlehem Steel had built huge ships, and things were busy. My Dad was a ship builder there then, and subsequently, for most of his life. He learned to be a skilled electrician but as the business changed, so did my father's job. When things were going well, Daddy was a foreman, but when business was slow he worked as a welder. It was then that he'd come home more exhausted and with a flashed red face.

When the union went on strike, it was difficult. Sometimes Daddy would sell things like tools or his jewelry to make enough money to feed us and to pay bills.

When I entered the third grade, I wanted to play the violin like my friend Charlie Castleman. My mother resurrected her father Geoffrey's violin and bought some strings for it. The school provided lessons, and the teacher told me that I picked it up easily. It took just three lessons for me to realize my mother was tormented by the sounds. During the strike at the shipyard cash was tight. So, my mother took advantage of the opportunity and sold the violin.

We had little money for commodities common to others. As my friends watched television, I enjoyed listening to "Ozzie and Harriet" on the radio, and unbeknownst to my parents, I hid the radio underneath my bed at night and turned down the volume to a whisper.

When Daddy became a supervisor, it was hard for him to endure labor strikes, because most of his friends were laborers, and he knew what they were going through. He also knew that he could quickly find himself on the other side when business slowed down. He was filled with relief at the end of a labor strike. Sometimes they were long and hard—but, somehow we always survived.

While my dad could walk to work from our apartment in The Point, in Braintree, he had to get up for work at five rather than six, in order to make the bus.

As a little girl, I walked to the bus stop precisely at 3:20PM to meet my father at the end of his workday. Other children waited for him as well. These same children loved him, and would even come to the house to ask him to come out to play.

His face lit up when he spotted us through the dirty window of the bus. He stepped off onto the pavement with the other workers—all were covered with dust from their work on the ship.

While it was in my father's nature to hug all of us, he didn't allow us to get too close to him when he came from work because of the asbestos and dirt that had accumulated on his clothes. He later learned that this was a very wise decision. Unknown to anyone at the time, asbestos would prove to be a serious carcinogen.

We all anticipated fun and frolic as we crossed the street and marched in song with my father to our dead-end road nearby. He was a pied piper, and to him every day was the Fourth of July. On some days the ice cream man would appear, and even during strikes, he would find money to buy treats for all of us.

Sometimes on Saturdays my father helped his father Sabatino build houses, and my brother Dick and I got to go along. This was an excuse for my father to be with his family that my mother would accept.

We didn't have a car at that time, so Pah came to pick us up in his truck. It was only a ten-minute ride.

Pah and his truck

When Pah arrived he usually came in for a cup of coffee before saying to my father, "OK—andiamo."

Dick and I would speed out the door and jump into the back of the open truck in anticipation of "a nice-a ride." We snuggled against the cab, wind whipping at our faces as the truck chugged along toward its destination. To us it was like being on an amusement park ride.

Chapter Six

At Mah and Pah's

On Sundays we frequently ate dinner at Mah and Pah's house. My mother appreciated those Sunday dinners on Edwards Street in the Point where she had learned to cook from Mah after she and my father had eloped.

When we arrived, Mah would usually be standing in front of the big black coal stove cooking. In the winter months, the heat of it warmed us as food sizzled, simmered, and baked at various stages of completion. With barely enough space for us all, we sat at the large enameled table in the kitchen as aunts and uncles sauntered in with their families.

By the time I was ten, I would be sent around the corner to the local bakery to buy bread for the meal. I'd hold my little brother's hand as we walked, and when we reached our destination, I guided him carefully away from the street and through the door. I took my jobs of caring for Dickie and buying bread very seriously.

In Rizzio's Bakery was to be found the bread that was everything to everybody—no cupcakes or fig squares—only bread.

"I'll have two loaves, please," I said, as I handed the baker the money that my father had given me. During our walk back to the house, we'd stop to pick up a bottle of carbonated Orangina for us grandchildren to drink during the meal.

By the time we arrived back at Edwards Street, around 2:30, the kitchen was full of relatives, and Mah had the first course of many ready to serve. We began with soup with little meatballs and escarole—a tradition. Using his metal cheese grater, Pah topped off each bowl with freshly ground Parmesan.

The meal always included pasta with sauce made of gold—dark red, grapefruit-sized tomatoes from Pah's garden. The traditional process of preparing the pasta was sacred. When Mah inherently knew the pasta was done to a perfect *al dente*, she instructed Pah to remove the huge boiling pot from the stove. He drained it until the last drop of water fell through the colander and down the drain. Then he poured the pasta into the large bowl that sat to the side of the hot burner. Mah gently poured her tomato sauce over the spaghetti (or rigatoni, or ziti) with a huge ladle, and mixed it with large wooden spoons until the last strand of pasta was suitably bathing in sauce. Then came the crown—a final coat of sauce and the Parmesan that Pah had waiting for her. Finally, Mah placed the heaping bowl in the middle of the table alongside a bottle of my grandfather Sabatino's homemade red table wine.

As Dick and I sipped our Orangina, someone always poured a little wine into our glasses to tone down the bubbles, and to give our drink a bit of a *kick*. Dick and I would sit quietly for the three-hour meal, and my aunts would inevitably reflect on our good behavior.

"Sandra and Richard are so well behaved," they would say as we sat *happy and mellow* in our chairs in the midst of emotional chaos.

For dessert we had Italian pastry—biscotti or rum cake—from the local pastry shop, and for the adults, dark black coffee boiled in a pan and strained, cup by cup, to capture the grounds that looked like wet dirt. My uncles spiked theirs with anisette.

Usually during the meal the battles began. Although they were of little consequence, they were loud and were fought as if all humanity depended on the outcome.

The gentle art of "reframing" was not a valued method of communication on Edwards Street. But, the confabulations in the debates were beyond even what a child could believe, and someone always had to be at fault for some insignificant event.

Blaming was the sport of the day. "Who let the fly in the house?" was a question that could start the revolution. When it was over, no consensus was reached, but everyone felt he or she had won. In addition, every family has someone who likes to light the fuse and then run, instigating chaos. Ours was relentless.

When the *meal* ended, the *arguing* ended, and everyone moved into the living room for the "no reason to celebrate, but we'll do it anyway" celebration.

FRONT: Dolores, Dickie, Sandra; BACK: Cookie (Egla), Rudy (Rudolpho), Mary, and Betty (Irma) – a few of the family after dinner

On holidays, chairs were lined against the walls and set between the sofas in anticipation of the festivities. Though it wasn't a large room, somehow there was *always* room for everyone. We children were *always* happy. As a little girl, my cousins and I had been constantly told how wonderful, smart, and beautiful we were. It didn't matter what the teacher or the neighbor or anyone else thought about us—when we were with *la famiglia*, we believed everything they told us, even if it wasn't true.

When Pah reached for his mandolin, the others followed his lead. Uncle Rudy balanced his accordion on his lap, my uncle Eddie (Aristide) stood ready with his guitar, and the music began.

All of the Pasquale's could sing and dance. Those who didn't play instruments would sing with great gusto because they all knew all the words to Italian songs that were happy, or romantic, or even funny—and there would be individual performances between choruses. I was almost always asked to sing a solo or a duet with one of my uncles. In addition to performing side-splitting impersonations, my father was an excellent singer and often sang with his sisters and brothers.

Pasquale Siblings: Willie, Pamp, Eddie,
Rudy, Mario, and Mary (Cerasoli)

Food was continually available so people could visit the kitchen if they needed a little fortification. The entertainments went on only until about 8 pm because people had to go to work the next day. On holidays the festivities began and ended later, sometimes well after midnight.

It wasn't unusual for us to spend time at my grandparents' on the weekends just "hanging out." Though the house was in the city, the back yard always felt like an Italian country garden because the grape arbor spanned the space above the door.

Beyond the house and through the coolness of the vines, we could see the vegetable garden and the shed at the edge of it. In the spring small lime green vines climbed over the arbor; when the leaves grew to fullness and turned dark green, it was like walking through a room as we moved out the back door and into the yard.

When the arbor matured, large plump, purple grapes hung down in clusters, and I would never miss an opportunity to pluck a bunch to share with my brother. They were wine grapes with big seeds in them, and Dick and I always had spitting contests to see who could blow them the farthest into the shrubs.

Pah grew huge tomatoes and eggplants and cucumbers. The garden and the arbor were a way of bringing his homeland with him.

Pah kept not only the holiday turkey in his neatly maintained shed, but also bunnies that turned into rabbits that turned into dinner. At first I didn't *connect the dots*, but it occurred to me one hot summer day that the cute little bunny I was playing with might end up on our dinner table.

While I had eaten rabbit many times at Sunday meals, and loved it, I vowed *that* day to never eat another piece of rabbit again. But my commitment only lasted until the next meal.

CHAPTER SEVEN

About Mom and Dad

My father had classic Italian features—black curly hair and a Roman nose. He was warm, passionate, volatile, fearless, and reckless in his generosity. While he was funny and easy to be with, he was not a man to cross.

Panfilio Pasquale

I once heard him talking about a stranger who had pulled a knife on him. He had offered the man a ride in our new car and agreed to take him to a certain location. But as they drove, the man insisted that my father take him to Boston. When he refused, the man held a knife to his face and demanded that he be driven to the city.

When Dad stopped at a red light, he rolled out of the car door, ran to the other side of the vehicle, and opened the passenger door. He grabbed the man, pulled the knife from his hand, and threw him to the ground. The man then ran in terror.

This experience was not enough to deter Pamp from picking up strangers thumbing rides; he never cared about what they looked like or what language they spoke.

Once, while my brother and I sat quietly in the back seat, he picked up a man who hopped into the front seat. Though the stranger looked like Charles Manson on a good day with his wild black hair sticking out everywhere—and even though he smelled really badly, he seemed very nice and expressed appreciation for the ride. This message of blindly accepting others carried into my future.

My father's instincts served him well, and as a result he usually got what he expected to get from others—it was almost always self-fulfilling.

Many things about my father drove my mother crazy, but she knew better than to try to change him. Sometimes Daddy would spontaneously invite friends for dinner; my mother learned to have extra food available at all times.

My mother Dorothy was a *lady*—a beautiful, anxious, and dignified woman with clear boundaries of what she considered reasonable behavior.

Dorothy Leet, 20 years old

While my father could make Mom laugh, she admitted she didn't have a particularly well-cultivated sense of humor. Though she was kind and generous in spirit, she had little patience for strangers in her car, or for neighborhood children banging on the door asking for "Pampy" to come out and play. My father exhausted her.

My parents always seemed to dance to a tune of aggravation, and while my mother often complained about my father's lack of boundaries, I sensed that she admired his free spirit and wished she could be like him. But they were very different people.

Dad's antics were difficult for my mother, who was often lost in the shadow of his personality. But one thing was always clear to me, my mother and father adored each other, and this made everything fine. While my mother deemed my dad careless and over confident about his ability to manage any situation, she always knew how very special he was.

CHAPTER EIGHT

Grandma Bessie

During the time we lived with Grandma Bessie my father was promoted to manager for the first time, and my parents were able to start saving money. Eventually, Grandma Bessie got a waitressing job and was able to spend the winters in Florida with her good friend, Kate.

One spring when Grandma Bessie returned from one of her winter stays in Florida, she announced that she had met someone. They planned to marry in the fall and live in Florida as husband and wife. Having been widowed for four years, she was ready for a new relationship.

Unfortunately she never made it to the altar. One night she left our house and never returned. A group of teenagers plowed into the car that she, her fiancé, and closest friend were traveling in, and she died almost instantly of a massive head injury. Her friend, Jewel, also suffered a severe head injury. In those days there were no such things as seat belts or a crime called *motor vehicle homicide*. Grandma's fiancé had minor injuries, but surely the accident left invisible scars.

When she died, Bessie was fifty-two years old—and from that moment—I believed that I too would die at the same age. I came to understand later that this was a consequence of grief.

As a child of ten I couldn't conceive of Grandma not coming home. I didn't cry; I couldn't. It was beyond my imagination that she was gone. Decades later, when I reached the ripe old age of fifty-three, I breathed a sigh of relief; I was still alive and healthy.

Years passed before I learned about my lost Aunt Eva; I heard as "a listening child" that Bessie had given away an infant at birth and when I asked my mother about it, she told me the story.

When Grandpa Geoffrey had contracted rheumatic fever in 1931, Bessie asked her parents in Canada to take care of their newborn daughter Eva until her husband regained his health. Bessie was forced to work in a factory because of Geoffrey's chronic illness; according to my mother, the family was so poor that it was embarrassing for her and her sisters. Once a year when the girls each received a pair of shoes from Good Will, they were usually calf-high and had to be cut down to the ankles with scissors, in order to fit.

Bessie's father William Rodger, and his wife Mary (Bessie's stepmother) agreed to take the new baby Eva so that Bessie could work. Mary had never had a child of her own; she was thrilled to have the opportunity to take care of a baby.

Though Geoffrey remained chronically ill, there were periods of time when he could travel to Canada with Bessie to visit her parents and their own infant daughter. Both Geoffrey and Bessie's parents lived in Nova Scotia and Geoffrey's Uncle Alex would fund the occasional trip to see Eva.

At first they hoped to take Eva home, but Mary had become deeply attached to her, and pleaded to have her stay with them for a while longer—and then a while longer again. "You can come from Massachusetts to see her, and we'll come to see you, but please don't take her," Mary pleaded.

Bessie had great love and respect for her stepmother, because Mary had always shown her great kindness. So, Bessie reluctantly "agreed." She never actually *said* "you can keep our daughter," but offered no resistance.

As a result of procrastination and Geoffrey's chronic illness, a bizarre charade ensued. Geoffrey and Bessie took their daughter out on day trips; no one tried to modify Eva's idea that they were just "nice friends of the family who loved children."

Eva was a young girl before she learned that William and Mary were *not* her parents, but in actuality her grandparents. When Eva was in junior high school a friend said to her, "What are you thinking? Can't you see that your mother and father are old? They *couldn't* be your parents."

I later learned first-hand that Eva ran home crying, hoping there was an explanation waiting in her mother's kitchen that would negate her conclusions. "Are you really my mother—tell me you are, tell me!" When she saw her mother's face, the answer was clear.

Mary had been totally taken off guard, and replied with a traditional answer, "I'll always be your mother, but you weren't born from my body."

My mother told me that there was little discussion about Eva in their house, but the family was always left with the impression that Eva was happy and much better off than they were.

My aunts and mother saw Eva periodically throughout the years. When their sister Eva came to visit with Bessie's parents, she wore new shoes and beautiful dresses. Her siblings envied her, believing that *she* was the *lucky* sister. They had continued to live in poverty for several years.

When Eva was a teenager she came with Mary and William to visit Bessie. By that time Eva knew that she'd been born a Leet and that the children she'd met in the past were her sisters and brother.

It was common years ago, and still today, for grandparents, relatives, and friends to raise children in the face of poverty and illness. It's hard to believe that Eva didn't feel rejected. After all, she was just a young girl and the only sister living apart from her family.

Grandma Bessie; her stepmother Mary (William's third wife); William; my Aunt Eva (biological daughter of Bessie, but raised by her grandparents, William and Mary)

CHAPTER NINE

Pah Dies

The Pasquale family was thriving. The usual schedule of parties, fun, and weddings prevailed.

Everything changed in 1955. Within months of Pah getting sick, a bed was set up in the dining room of their house on Edwards Street in The Point, and a nurse was hired to take care of him. While my aunts readily took care of Mah, who was consumed with thyroid disease and a resulting dementia, personal care privacy issues made it impossible for them to care for their father as well.

On the night our family assembled to be with Pah, his last words to me had been, "Don't get any taller." I was still a young teen and Pah was just an inch taller than I.

My cousin Dolores and I were sent up to the bedroom where my aunts had slept in their youth. We left Dolores's mother (Aunt Mary), my father, and a group of other relatives at Pah's side. The smell of tomato sauce simmering permeated the air as I walked up to the cold bedroom.

When Dolores and I woke up on the following morning, my grandfather was gone. Frost on both sides of the windows in the bedroom made exquisite designs on the glass as the light shown into the room. As we snuggled under multiple layers of quilts, we talked about Pah, and Dolores said, "My father could die, too." Her dad, my Uncle Benny, had experienced a serious stroke a couple of weeks before, and was in the hospital. Dolores visited her father after school every day, and knew that he was significantly compromised. She was told that he could die, but it was difficult for us to fathom death at our young ages. This was new territory for us.

Pah's wake was held at the local funeral parlor, our family's undertaker. It seems that the family was more interested in having an *Italian* undertaker than a *good* one. The fragrance of the roses (lining the perimeter of the room from all those people Pah had helped during his lifetime) was overpowering.

Until I saw my grandfather laid out in that beautiful wooden coffin with roses draped over it, I'd never been to a wake or seen a dead body. I loved my grandfather dearly, but I felt nothing for a long time.

In 1955, Italian wakes and funerals, like weddings, demanded gestures that, outside the culture, might be viewed as inappropriate. It was commonplace to see people crying and screaming—and relatives falling onto caskets—the sign of ultimate respect.

I was sitting quietly in the corner when the door of the crowded room of the funeral home flew open, and Tootsie, my father's cousin from Chicago, came sprinting down the aisle. I was in awe. She ran, screaming, "Poor, poor, Uncle Sam!"

As she took a dramatic dive onto my grandfather's casket, her white fur coat flared around her in the air. She landed on the large spread of roses, the coat finally resting like a large dead animal on the crushed flowers. I was horrified as I sat like a statue in the back of the room. Her brother Frankie and two of my uncles pulled Tootsie up and off the casket and guided her to her mother, Aunt Bianca, who, by then, was standing nearby with her sister— Grandma Emma and daughter Geraldine.

Eventually I felt Pah's loss profoundly. He was a well-built man of about five feet three inches, and a quiet force. His kindness was not ostentatious, rather softly present. Pah had held his family together during the most difficult of times. Working as a mason and contractor, he had fed his own family and helped many of Emma's nine siblings through the Great Depression.

Pah always seemed preoccupied with his work, or the garden and house, or with other responsibilities. We weren't close in a traditional way, but I felt akin to my grandfather's nature in a way that made me feel and care about people in the same way he did; he was a generous person and, by nature, a very good man.

Only once do I recall questioning my grandfather's kindness; I was four years old. The day before Thanksgiving I was at his house on Edwards Street in The Point. I quietly—and secretly—followed Pah to the basement, which was empty but for a table under the cellar window and a store of bottled homemade red wine and grappa against the wall. Light shown from the window onto a hatchet lying on the table. Pah picked it up and examined the blade.

A huge turkey was meandering around the basement. Within minutes my grandfather chased the bird, caught it, and held it securely under his arm as it twisted and squirmed in every direction. Getting a good grip, he pressed the turkey's head to the table and struck its neck with a fierce blow of the hatchet. Blood sprayed all over the clean floor of the basement.

Fear ran through me and I put my face into my hands. *The poor, poor thing, how could my nice grandfather cut the turkey's head off?*

Once the deed was done, the turkey fell to the floor with its head hanging from its neck. I watched in horror as the turkey miraculously turned right-side up and began to run around the staircase until, once again, it dropped to the floor.

When Pah spotted me, he had already drained the remaining blood from the poor creature into a bucket that had been placed under the table, had tucked our main course under his arm with its head hanging to one side, and was heading up the stairs. Surprisingly, he had little reaction to my being there. To him it was life.

He took the turkey upstairs and Mah plucked it and jammed it into the ice box.

The next day, Mah prepared the turkey for cooking. When she attempted to put it into the oven of the big black coal stove, it barely fit. Pah had fed it for weeks before the day of its demise, so it was a huge God-damned bird when it met its fate.

We all sat down to Thanksgiving dinner. First we ate soup and pasta. Pah could barely hold up the platter as he placed the turkey on the table to be carved—the turkey was *that* heavy.

For only a moment did I think of the headless bird running around the basement. The aroma of the freshly cooked turkey, and the fact that it had turned from a limp dead bird to a crisp brown succulent course in our Thanksgiving dinner allowed me to forget the horror of the previous day. "I'll have a leg," I uttered, as Pah began to carve and pull the turkey apart. As I held the drumstick in my hand and thought about the day before, I had a new appreciation of the sacrifice the bird had made for me. Had I not been my grandfather's granddaughter, I might not have been able to consume it with delight and satisfaction.

CHAPTER TEN

Another Death

Only two months had passed when Uncle Benny died. He'd been in the hospital for several months after suffering a debilitating stroke. My cousin Dolores had been my only "sister," and we were very close.

When Uncle Gaetano (Guy) was sent to drive her and her brother Robert Angelo to our grandparents' house where the extended family was gathering, he flatly informed the two children that they had better be strong because their father had just died. Dolores and Bobby sat in the back seat stunned and devastated.

My great uncle Guy Faiella wasn't the "sharpest tack in the box." He'd consumed a bottle of creosol one night thinking it was whiskey, and then blamed his wife for trying to kill him. He was nearly blinded by the experience, but continued to drive his car as if he had 20/20 vision.

These months had indeed been such a sad time for our family.

Angelo (Uncle Benny) Cerasoli

CHAPTER ELEVEN

Childhood Challenges

By the time I'd reached my early teens, I was suffering from a negative self-image that would take me decades to understand. In my very early years, I had been deemed smart, but, by the time I started school, my memory had faded to the point where it affected my ability to learn to read. Perhaps I had a learning disability or maybe the lead paint I had chewed on the windowsills next to my bed in The Point and in Braintree had damaged my growing brain. In those days the paint contained lead which later proved to be very detrimental, and no one then much considered such things as learning disabilities.

"It's your turn to read, Sandra," Miss Penny, my first grade teacher, said to me. "Please stand and read aloud." I could feel my face flush as I shifted from one foot to the other. It was a merciless request and I limped from word to word. I could feel the impatience around me, and I felt stupid and humiliated.

On the day I brought my first report card home, my mother was next door in my aunt's apartment in The Point; I wasn't supposed to, but I opened it. Both my conduct and progress were bad. While I didn't ever act out in class, I talked continually to distract others from my stupidity—thus the "U"—unsatisfactory conduct.

I cried "deep and hard" as I anticipated my mother coming in and seeing proof of my failure on the page. I had always been smart, and now I was just a "bad, dumb, little girl."

My mother was not happy when she saw my grades, and my father's disappointment was visceral. They told me that they had expected more. *Why?* I thought, *I can't read and I'm not very smart.*

While school never came easy to me, I could carry a tune, and people liked the way I sang. Music had been central to the life of our family. Voices, guitars, mandolins, dancing—they were all central. I learned from an early age to use music as a drug. It calmed me and made me happy.

When I was in the first grade I got the role as the Virgin Mary in the school play because I could sing and knew all the words to "Away in the Manger." In sixth grade I was the lead dancer on stage during the school performance because the teacher said I was the best dancer in the class.

Once when I was eleven I went on "Community Auditions," a performance competition TV show. The winner was determined by mailed-in votes from viewers. "One-person-one-vote" was a concept my family did *not* understand. My mother said that because of their voting exuberance, I was disqualified, and 1st place went to a jump rope act.

Someone in the viewing audience saw me on television and offered me free voice lessons, which I declined because my father thought I didn't need them.

Singing was my passion and my father was forever teaching me to sing Italian songs. Once while I was at Aunt Betty's house, my father stood me in front of Cousin Frankie Fratto from Chicago, and prompted me to sing "Mama" in Italian. I was not comfortable with Cousin Frankie; we rarely saw him.

"Not bad for someone who doesn't speak the language," my father bragged in jest. My dark skin and eyes, and curly dark hair made me resemble a child on the streets of Italy, and though I didn't speak Italian, I could memorize the songs in the language and without an accent.

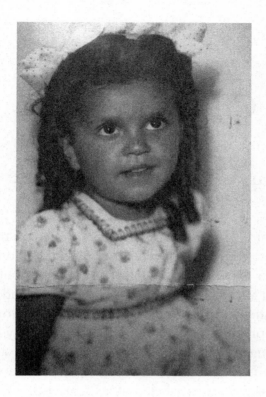

Sandra Pasquale at six years

Later, my father's Uncle Rudolpho taught me to play nine chords on the guitar. I was told throughout my life that I could sing with style and passion even though my range was only a little more than an octave.

By the time I was in high school I was sometimes asked to sing at events, and when I graduated I was chosen the most talented girl in my class of 350 students. I loved melodies of all kinds and often won talent competitions.

While I always seemed like a happy and even a joyful person to everyone around me, I was only happy in the midst of music or Pasquale relatives who loved music. This meant that I was actually sad most of that time.

Chapter Twelve

Growing Up Easy, "Feeling Life Hard"

Adolescent hormonal changes cause a rollercoaster of feelings and mine were translated into feelings of sadness for anyone and everyone who experienced bad fortune. For as long as I could remember I'd felt that everyone's pain was mine, and that I didn't deserve to be happy while there were people in the world who were suffering. Impractical maybe, but it was how I truly felt.

The feelings of inadequacy that had emerged as a result of my memory issues in elementary school were re-enforced in high school when I was labeled as a "scatter-brain" by my *very smart* friends who had no idea what it was like to be me. Spelling issues discouraged me from writing; being unable to remember multiplication tables sealed the deal in math; and having difficulty remembering facts killed any interest I might have had in history or science. In those days there were no such things as spell check or calculators, and there was only one way to be taught anything.

While I couldn't remember many things, there were areas that for some reason had been fine-tuned from the very beginning. I've always been able to remember events from my very early childhood; my mother always told me that she couldn't believe how clear my visual images were. Though it took me longer than most to remember people's names, I could remember details about who they were, and what their lives had been like. I also understood people and my instincts carried me forward. Because I remembered everything that happened to people, what they liked or didn't like, and because I generally liked almost everyone, I always had many friends. They, however, had no idea I was feeling inadequate and that it weighed like an anvil on my heart.

As a teen I got by in school, but I didn't expect to ever rise above my short-comings. In essence, I gave up without realizing it. In the end, I could have done so much more.

Fortunately, I did have my music. I'd started a band with two of my girl friends. And I was the lead singer, and only female, in a rock n' roll group from the next town. We played in local clubs, and at our high school, and Father Dallinger let us rehearse in the function hall at Emmanuel Episcopal Church in Braintree.

Because I appeared to be "not all that smart," my parents focused on my looks and talent. While people told me I was pretty, all *I* could see was how beautiful the young women around me were. Like many teenage girls, I thought I was overweight, and one pimple could ruin my day.

In essence I didn't feel very good about myself. Nonetheless, my parents convinced me to compete in a local beauty pageant. After I found out I'd won, I stood on the stage like a deer in the headlights.

When I got to the state competition, I chose not to smile at the judges the way my parents had told me to. I felt embarrassed and almost rebellious, and didn't want to look like I expected to be chosen—it made no sense. As I walked onto the stage I looked at the judges with a stone-faced glare. *Don't smile, don't smile,* the voice in my head kept saying.

When I got home my parents were mad. "You would have won with a smile," my mother said. "Why didn't you smile?" I just shrugged.

I came in second, and that got me a scholarship to charm school—just what I needed—another vote for vanity.

Every aspect of my teen years was invested in my objectification. A little voice in my head kept saying, *you're not pretty enough to catch a handsome and rich husband so you can become a good little wife and mother.* That's the way it was for many girls when I was growing up—there was only one goal.

If all your friends are smart and you don't feel smart; and you win a beauty contest and have no idea why, it's more of an embarrassment than an honor to carry that title. If you're an Episcopalian when the rest of your large family is Catholic, you don't know where you fit in. And I most surely felt I didn't.

Chapter Thirteen

Nursing School Friends

Because I cared about people and was a nurturer; and because my father was *dead set against* me becoming a nurse because I'd be seeing naked bodies, I applied to *several* nursing schools. I was fortunate to get into a nursing program in a decent hospital school near Boston, in spite of my average high school performance.

While in nursing school, I became close to several young women, and each would teach me something useful. My good friend Arlene Klapman took me home with her on weekends now and then, and the Klapmans treated me like a member of their large Jewish family.

I loved Arlene's parents, and her sister, aunts, and uncles. I loved hearing stories about her grandmother Bubbie, who, at eighty years old, had climbed up a ladder and into the second story window after accidently getting locked out of the house.

Bubbie spoke Yiddish and referred to cars as machines, and drunks as "hookaholics." Once her grandson Joseph, after learning a bit of Spanish in school, asked her how she was. "Como esta usted, Bubbie?"

Bubbie replied seriously and with sadness, "Oh no! Perry Como is dead? Venn did he die?"

In addition to my good friend Arlene, there was Claire. We'd been casual acquaintances at Braintree High School, and became closer friends in our first year of nurses' training.

In the summer Claire and I visited her grandfather on Cape Cod. His cottage was primitive, but perfect. Her Grandpa was an

Irishman with a twinkle in his eye and a quick wit. He knew that we'd lied about our ages to get into Joe's, the local joint in town, but didn't think twice about it. When the moon was full, he'd say "They'll be bloodshed down Joe's tonight!" And then he'd chuckle with us.

Joe's was a classic kind of local dive, and the first place I'd seen black and white people dance together. I don't recall ever being told it was a *bad* thing, but I knew it was something you didn't see every day in America.

Helen Hennesian, another good friend from nursing school, was a recent immigrant from Lebanon. While I'd never cared much about such history or politics—or much of anything for that matter—I cared about Helen.

Her father's family had been affected by the Armenian holocaust in 1921, and her father subsequently moved to Lebanon where he married and had two daughters. The family grew up near Beirut in a village where Jews, Muslims, and Christians lived peacefully together. Their family was Christian.

After Helen and her sister graduated from high school, her father was determined to have them come to America. He was an intellectual who felt that America could offer his daughters a better education, but he wasn't wealthy. He had saved enough to send his family to the States, and planned to join them later, but he never came.

I learned from Helen almost accidentally. She was from a different world, and I wanted to know more about it.

Helen laughed easily, and at one point we told her that the medical term for the word flatus (intestinal gas) was called farts, so she proceeded to document it that way in the hospital on patients' records. This was a source of amusement for days.

Helen was a "born again" Christian who hoped to meet a preacher and marry him. Ultimately she married a Jewish man and had two boys, but not before she brought me to the Tremont Temple Baptist Church in Boston, where we both were indoctrinated to the glory of Jesus Christ.

On my first visit to Boston with Helen, I got *saved*. It was a bizarre turn of events for me. I became a born-again Christian in an intense and highly intolerant religious sect. In the process, I took up with Bob Marsh, who was an upstanding member of the youth group associated with the church and an upwardly mobile college senior at Harvard who was heading to Harvard Law School in the fall.

I felt like a fool as we collectively bowed our heads in various public places across the city, but I was swept up in the fervor of it all, so I did it anyway. As an evangelist, I prayed aloud at McDonald's with Bob and his friends. Just as easily, we could have exercised our dedication to Jesus privately, but the spectacle of it was at least half of the intent. Young minds are so easy to capture, and mine was prime.

Bob wanted to marry and take me to his family in Texas for a life of prayer and opulence. While he talked about me *meeting* his parents, he wanted to stay as *far away* from my family as possible. Young and insecure, I felt patronized when I was with Bob—he was so *conservative* that I always felt the intensity of my *Pasquale* name.

My parents were concerned, and with good reason. The revelation of the Holy Spirit mandated that I pull away from my parents who were *not* born again in God's eyes, even though my mother was a devout Christian who'd lived a life worthy of respect, and my father's love for life and others was superior to anyone I'd ever known.

Bob's college dormitory was next to Eliot House where my good friend Paul Pimentel resided, and my boyfriend was often appalled at the drunken and irreverent antics of Paul and his roommates. While all of these "derelicts" would ultimately become prominent and successful doctors, lawyers, politicians, and financiers, Bob Marsh viewed them as "a boorish and irreverent bunch of hooligans," and he didn't understand how I could have friends such as these.

Bob was a snob; he asked me to give up my *tennis shoes* (sneakers), because they "weren't very nice." In those days everyone my age wore sneakers like mine, and I couldn't understand why this bothered him. I'd given up enough for Bob—my friends, my life—but I drew the line at my favorite tennis shoes.

Bob's parents owned a fancy department store in Dallas, and I'm sure he would have been embarrassed for me to meet them while wearing my white-washed tennis shoes. Fortunately, I never went to Texas.

CHAPTER FOURTEEN

Intervention

When Bob left for his Reserve Military Training in the summer of 1962, Paul Pimentel felt compelled to "save me from being saved."

"This relationship is a bad idea," Paul said. "You can't love a guy like him; it's impossible. You've been totally hooked by his good looks and money, and by those "nut cakes" in Boston, the narrow-minded religious bigots who think they sit on the right hand of the Father—and by the way, you're wacked out, too."

In spite of Paul's proclamation, I continued to go to the church in Boston over the summer, and in fact, attended a retreat in Maine to reaffirm my commitment to Jesus. During one of the sessions when I talked about helping a non-English speaking man find his way in the subway station, one of the workshop participants asked, "Well, was he a *Christian*?"

I answered quickly, "What would Jesus have done?"

As brain-washed as I was, I knew that the girl's question was unkind and crazy, and it served as a red flag for the insanity of the entire experience. But I hung in.

Paul's persistence during the summer of 1962 helped me to see that my relationship with the Texan would not lead to a marriage made in heaven.

At first I'd thought that anyone with a degree from Harvard must know more than I, but then realized that it meant little in the absence of common sense. While I knew Bob wasn't a bad fellow,

I felt he was as misguided as I. And most importantly, I realized that I could never love someone who didn't understand tolerance.

Bob's indoctrination had begun when he was a small child, so it might be unlikely he'd ever be able to see things differently—even with a fancy education. The relationship was over.

As soon as I ended my courtship with Bob, Paul quietly admitted that he loved me. I wasn't ready to do the same, and in time, his friends told him to give up.

He didn't.

CHAPTER FIFTEEN

Propose and Compromise

Paul and I had been connected (in one way or another) for eight years, and in 1963 he asked me to marry him. We'd been thirteen years old when we'd met in the hallway at school, and our friendship had served as the foundation of a relationship that would sustain us both for a lifetime.

Seven years after we met, and several months after his pronouncement of love for me, I realized I couldn't possibly live without him. When he got down on one knee and asked me to marry him, I said yes.

He *wasn't* the Lone Ranger, but I *loved* him.

At the end of Paul's junior year of college, we carefully made plans to tell our parents (in particular, his father Fred) about our plans to marry. In his usual fashion, Paul was armed with facts to convince his father that it would work. He never got to present them.

We decided to tell my parents first, and suspected it would be easy. Besides, with their history, my parents weren't about to give us a bad time.

"Are you sure you know what you're doing?" they asked.

We said we were.

I was happy that they loved Paul and that *they* were happy with *my* choice; I was twenty-two years old—and in those days, it was considered high time to be a bride.

We were sure Paul's parents would be another story. Paul was still in college—and it was likely that his father Fred had hoped for a different bride for his only son. Fred considered *everyone* to be beneath him, even the Portuguese—and he *himself* was Portuguese.

Fred was an engineer and often consulted for paper mills in Maine. On Friday nights in the summer, he would bring large lobsters home to Braintree for dinner. It was understood that Paul would bring me home with *him* to share in the feast.

As we came into the kitchen of Paul's house, my future father-in law was pulling two-pound lobsters out of a pot of boiling water and landing them on paper plates that had been placed on the newspaper covered table.

Paul's parents, his two sisters, and Paul and I all cracked the lobsters and dipped chunks of meat into copious amounts of butter. There was a silent tension as we ate.

I had come to the conclusion that Fred *liked* me, but I knew he *hated the idea* of me. As I sat and ate dinner with his little family, I remembered that my name was Sandra *Pasquale*—and shamefully—I was sorry for it.

I had graduated from nursing school and I was shocked when I passed the nurses exam on the first shot. When I became an RN, I got a job at the New England Baptist Hospital in Boston in the operating room. We'd arrived at Paul's house armed and ready with facts about my salary, the cost of an apartment, and about how much to allocate for every need as a married couple. Even my pantyhose had been included in our budget.

Upon the revelation of our intent to marry, Fred did something that was rare in their house—he exploded. He could neither deny nor control, so he lost all reason, and broke into a rage. I think he thought I was pregnant, but that was impossible. I was a good Italian girl. Even when he realized I wasn't pregnant, it didn't matter. He just kept ranting.

Paul's mother Dorothy said a few words softly and then went off to the living room. She probably agreed with her husband, but she was too much of a lady to get involved in the havoc. Paul's sister Susan never revealed her feelings on the matter; she just got the hell out of there, and I didn't blame her. Paul's younger sister Joanie also left the room, but came back several times to stand up to her father on our behalf; she was swiftly chased out of the kitchen each time. I had to admire her courage and good will. She'd always be better at fighting for others than she was for herself.

Paul tried to reason with his father at first, but he eventually stormed outside in frustration, and walked up and down the driveway leaving me *alone* in the kitchen with Fred.

Fred made me feel like I was being accused of bringing the family to impending doom, and as he ranted on, I shrunk into my seat. He paced back and forth in short runs in the small kitchen. "Do you understand that I pray for that boy every night? Do you understand?"

Fred's life was predictable and safe and remained organized because he kept it that way. He expected the same for his son. You grow, you go to college, you get a job, and *then* you get married. Doing anything out of sequence was beyond his comprehension,

On the other hand, *I* never did *anything* in sequence or in the same way twice. This proved to be the bottom line of our incompatibility. I knew it was useless to try to make any kind of statement or plea, so I continued to sit still for fear of agitating Fred further.

How can Paul just leave me here with his father's nastiness? I asked myself, as I sat at the kitchen table. While I'd been trained by the Pasquale's to argue with the best of them, Fred paralyzed me.

When Fred finally left the room, I joined Paul in the driveway. We drove away from the house in total dismay, but we had no reason to be shocked; Fred's reaction had been completely predictable.

During the following days I thought hard about our engagement, and admitted to myself that getting married early was not the best idea. Paul would be going to Vietnam after graduation. In the meantime, we probably could have made it financially on my nurse's salary, but Paul wouldn't have been able to become a naval officer because, at that time, ROTC candidates entering active duty had to be single.

Furthermore, a pregnancy could have been difficult to manage. And enough resistance and bad feeling had built up to ruin our wedding day. I wanted *better*.

"I don't think we should get married, Paul. This all feels terrible to me. I want things to be *right*; I want a beautiful wedding with happy people. Let's wait until you graduate."

Paul was silent for a minute, and then said, "OK. I guess you're right. We'll wait. But my father needs to promise he won't cause any more problems after the year passes."

I knew I'd let him off the hook with his dad, and that was OK with me.

In spite of the fact that his son was marrying a girl Fred considered to be beneath him, he promised to honor Paul's wishes and to accept our wedding after Paul graduated.

My relationship with Fred would always be complicated. While he was far from perfect, he had an endearing warmth and love for his family that I envied and wished to be a part of. Perhaps this is what drove me to be compliant and allowed me to love him—anyway.

During our two-year engagement while Paul was in college, he tried to make money so that we wouldn't be starting life with debt. He asked his housemaster John Finley if he could use the kitchen in the basement of Eliot House at Harvard to cook burgers and the like for students during off hours when the dining room was closed. "I'll call it *The Eliot House Grill* and they'll love it," Paul explained, "and I can give my roommates jobs." Master Finley was a likable and dignified intellectual, with a rather affected demeanor, the kind of man you would *expect* to find at Harvard.

"Yes, you can use the kitchen in the basement for your restaurant, but you need to share it."

Julia Child cooked for the Harvard Fellows once a month, and on the few occasions that Paul had seen her, she'd been dramatic and "testy." Understandably, she demanded a spotless kitchen; occasionally Paul would delay cleaning until the last minute.

When standards fell, Julia carried on with intent. "Get out of my kitchen," she yelled, as she tossed things about in a snit.

When she complained to Master Finley about the abomination in the kitchen, the Master responded with a plea. "Paul, can't you use your considerable charm to keep 'the French woman' happy?"

"She doesn't think I'm charming. She doesn't like me—at *all,*" Paul said.

The sanitation in the restaurant was *less than perfect*; the local Department of Public Health (DPH) told Paul that his utensils had a higher germ count than the then polluted Charles River. Possibly, they were looking for some kind of pay-off, but Paul was unwilling to entertain such a thought, so we never knew the true extent of the contamination. Paul decided to outwit the "crooks" by making it impossible to fail the DPH standards.

Then the cleaning began! I helped Paul wash down everything in the restaurant with bleach—twice; the floors, walls, and surfaces were completely scrubbed and wiped until there was little opportunity for any bacteria to survive. I then took every cooking utensil to the hospital and sterilized them. When I got back to the kitchen, I opened the packages of spoons, knives, and forks using sterile technique, and replaced them gently into the bleached, stainless steel drawer.

It would have been unlikely that the inspectors had ever seen a restaurant as clean; when they returned, we were ready. They took slides and cultures. When it was over Paul said, "The unscrupulous bastards told me I barely passed the inspection. But without bacteria, they couldn't shut me down, and they couldn't ask for a bribe, either!"

From the day The Grill opened with a menu of burgers and Paul's mother's pies and scrumptious chocolate squares (that sold like hotcakes), lines formed until late into the night. The license to operate The Grill would allow us to enter marriage in a much more stable financial state. Paul didn't hear a word from Julia Child ever again.

The year before we got married was uneventful, but for the episode with my car. I'd been working for about a year when I bought a five-year old, white MG convertible, and it was really quite sharp. Paul loved that car and he resolved its initial problems during the course of the year: he tuned the carburetor monthly, reground the valves, put in a new exhaust system—in other words, it was *his* baby.

I hated driving in Boston and had no place to park near the hospital. I also needed to be a contortionist to drive it; the seat was stuck in a position that didn't allow me to easily reach the pedals; I needed to put a huge pillow behind me.

So, Paul kept the car in Cambridge near his dorm, opting to pay the parking tickets in return for the pleasure of driving the MG all week. Fine with me. During the week, I lived at the New England Baptist Hospital dormitory in Boston, so Paul picked me up on Fridays and dropped me off on Sunday nights.

The car was running like a top and we expected it to be *our car* after we got married. But our plans changed.

One day while Paul was helping our good friend Jerry Goldberg repair the roof of his house, he noticed the MG moving down the street. He wondered where I was going, but then he realized I wasn't in it.

When I heard the commotion, I ran out and saw Paul jump off the roof and run toward the street. A boy was running next to my car while trying to get into it. "How do I get in the car?" the boy asked anxiously.

"Slide the window open, and find the string in the door under it, and then pull the rope."

"What! Rope? String?"

The boy had no idea what to do, and it's a good thing that he didn't. The car escaped the boy and hugged the curb all the way down the street. Paul ran after it and held his head in disbelief at the end of the road as the little MG plowed through a fence, bounced up in the air, and flew off a twenty-foot cliff into a ravine.

Before I reached the end of the road, Paul ran around the embankment to where the car had landed and looked in horror as it teetered like a seesaw on a huge cement pipe. Fortunately, the gas tank remained intact.

Neighbors joined Paul at the bottom of the ravine. I remained on the upper road looking down at the group staring at my car.

At first Paul stood in disbelief. But when reality hit, he began to yell and jump up and down like a mad man; when he spotted me on the hill he didn't hold back. "What the hell! How could you?"

I had neglected to put the car in gear or to secure the emergency brake.

I can't explain it, but when I saw him carrying on, I began to laugh, and the more I laughed, the more infuriated he got.

Miraculously, the group of large men collectively lifted the car off the cement culvert; it was Herculean.

Surprisingly, the major structures of the vehicle were preserved, but much of the floor in the front seat was gone. Paul was able to drive the car around the embankment and back to the road.

On this day I realized there's an almost spiritual connection between men and cars. To me it was just a car; to Paul it was a friend who had a near-death experience. I had insurance, so it wasn't the end of life as we knew it, but to Paul this was life-altering.

As we drove home from Jerry and Jane's house, the freezing air and fumes blew in our faces from the gaping hole in the floor between us; Paul sulked and refused to talk to me.

We had the hole patched and the car was repainted a beautiful bronze by the time we were married.

Mah had slowly become bedridden and had dementia. The only words she could remember were Italian swear words which allowed her to tell people to go away and leave her alone.

Prior to Paul's and my wedding, and in the *Italian family tradition*, my father had threatened to strike from the invitation list the name of every person who had neglected to visit Mah during the previous twelve years. My father didn't need a notebook to keep track; cousins and friends who had neglected his mother were all susceptible to his threats.

I fought with him aggressively about his vindictive snit, and as usual he won the battle and lost the war. When it came to arguing he couldn't be matched. Paul was always amazed that at the end of every battle he had with my father, he, himself, would end up arguing my father's position, and my father his. Somehow my father was always right.

During the debates over who would be invited to our wedding we both said some nasty things to each other, but again, *in the Italian tradition*, he invited *everyone*—all 350 of them.

When the wedding invitations were being printed, I asked my mother about her long lost sister Eva and suggested that she write and invite her to the wedding.

My mother instantly responded. "Yes, I'll definitely write. I should have thought of it myself." After sitting quietly for a moment my mother took a pen and began writing:

> Dear Eva,
>
>   My daughter Sandra is getting married on June 20th and we would all love to have you come to her wedding. You have a wonderful family here, and we want you to be part of it . . .

The wedding ceremony was uneventful but for the fact that Paul had to forage on his hands and knees to find the ring that our best man Rae had dropped on the floor at the absolute worst possible moment.

Paul and I stood in front of the altar in the Episcopal Church where I'd grown up and I don't think Father Dallenger had ever seen so many Catholics and Jews in his sanctuary.

Umpteen bridesmaids and groomsmen stood erect with their bright pink gowns and white tuxedos that had been chosen to blend with Paul's dress white Navy uniform. It was quite wonderful.

Paul and Sandy get married

The reception was at a local country club, and everyone was happy. My parents gave me a royal wedding in spite of the fact that they didn't have much money.

Our wedding (as is typical of any large family event) brought together the close-knit relatives who lived close to one another and saw each other frequently, as well as those who lived at a distance and rarely visited.

We arrived at the country club ready for a party, but first there were the formalities. My aunts—Barbara, Peggy, and Mary—had been making a fuss in the corner. There was someone else with them.

Suddenly, what had been a perfunctory task on my part became exciting, and then—moving. I instantly recognized the face in front of me without ever having met the person behind it. My long lost Aunt Eva was standing with her husband at her side, and I knew it was she without a single word.

I hugged her and told her that I was thrilled they had come, that it was like having my grandmother in front of me.

Eva was a gentle person who couldn't harbor an angry thought. In later conversations she would tell me about growing up with her stodgy old father (grandfather) and how he hadn't felt like a father to her. I remembered him as cold and distant like my grandfather Geoffrey, so this didn't surprise me.

While Eva hadn't felt close to her father, she talked about having had the most wonderful mother in the world.

While I loved all my mother's sisters and my Uncle Geoff (who was more like my older brother), I recognized the sweet innocence about Eva that made her unique. Perhaps in some ways she *was* the lucky one.

Mah had been one of ten children. Her older sister, Aunt Bianca Fratto lived in Chicago, and had eight children. Bianca would sometimes come to Quincy to visit her siblings. When she came to Braintree, my mother would cook for her. Bianca acknowledged that it was rare to see a non-Italian who could cook, but conceded that her sister (Mah) had successfully taught my Scottish mother how to cook *Italian*.

Though the culture in the Chicago family was different than that of our local relatives, we all shared important values; children and family were *everything* to *all* of us. At least one Fratto would represent that branch of the family at each of our east coast weddings and funerals.

Though Luigi (Lou) and Frankie Fratto hung out in their Chicago club with Sammy Davis, Jr., Frank Sinatra, Jimmy Durante, and Vic Damone, and many other celebrities, my father, his siblings and his Quincy cousins did not join them in spite of an open invitation. It would take front-row seats to see their friend Rocky Marciano compete for the title for heavyweight boxing champion of the world to lure my father and others in his family to Chicago for a whirlwind 24-hour visit. Rocky had met many of my cousins in Quincy because he lived in Brockton, and was much admired.

The arrival of the Frattos was always eventful, but this time Paul and I were too caught up with the wedding to take note. When the Chicago cousins came into the party, their limo was parked outside, and two men wearing black suits and Fedoras hovered outside the door.

Frankie approached the reception line. He moved slowly with a quiet calm as he smiled ever so slightly. His pleasant round face was compelling, and his missing ear seemed to add to his charm. He shook Paul's hand, kissed him on both cheeks, and whispered in his ear, "You come to Chicago, we'll take care of you," while handing him a thick envelope. Frankie kissed me on both cheeks and then went on to make a fuss over my father.

At most weddings, the bride dancing with her father is a *special* moment, but at Italian weddings, it's *monumental*. When the time for the special dance arrived, there was great tension in the room. My father had taught me to dance as soon as I could walk, and as we glided across the dance floor at the reception, people began to weep openly. Of course, the Pasquales, Faiellas, Pettinellis, Cappolas, Cifunis, Frattos, and Sandonatos cried harder than the others. Cousin Frankie wiped his eyes with a white handkerchief, and most everyone who stood around my father and me in a circle shed a few tears.

As my father and I danced, the band sapped through "Daddy's Little Girl." While I had a huge lump in my throat and a few tears snuck out, my father broke down into choking sobs.

Daddy's little girl

To my father, "Daddy's Little Girl" was more than a song. While we often argued, I knew he would do anything for me. In the year prior to the wedding, a prowler had been peeping through my bedroom window at night. The large footprints in the dirt outside were evidence that a large man had been lurking there. Because it was around the time that the Boston Strangler was ravaging young nurses, my parents had been extremely nervous.

My father called the police and demanded that they put someone outside to watch the house. They minimized the threat. "If you don't do it, I will—and if the bastard shows up, I'll shoot him," my father had proclaimed.

"Don't do that, Mr. Pasquale, you going to jail won't help your daughter. We'll send a patrol car by frequently, but we can't case the place all night."

When my father borrowed a rifle, one of our neighbors was concerned that Dad would spend his life in jail, so he stayed under a bush with him for two nights.

When the bastard *did* show up, I heard two shots, and thought my father was destined for incarceration.

Fortunately, as my father had taken dead aim at the prowler, our neighbor pulled the gun to the side which caused the bullets to miss the Peeping Tom. A large man ran through the open field behind our house and disappeared. Though the police were unable to find him, he'd never returned. My father had accomplished his mission and—thanks to our neighbor—had remained a free man.

Our family remained proper and polite throughout the wedding. They danced and had fun. But some of the more spontaneous guests would wait to cut loose at the *after party* on Holden Road, after the *pinched people* went home.

While Paul's side of the family had sent blankets and toasters, my relatives gave cash that was viewed as a measurement of admiration and respect. This is the unspoken Italian way.

All the money gifts were taken to the back room for safekeeping. While my father always liked to give money rather than take it, his curiosity and concern got the better of him at the reception, so he slipped into the back room to make sure the gifts were safe.

When he saw how generous his family had been, he was shocked. He worried that his siblings had gone too far, but was moved by their generosity. Frankie's envelope alone contained $1,000 in 20-, 50-, and 100-dollar bills. This was almost the cost of the entire wedding in 1965.

I'd been on autopilot for my entire wedding. Paul's only thought was to get me away and to bed. I hadn't ever been to *bed* with him and his loins were aching. My father had made it quite clear that I would remain a *good Italian girl* and stay chaste until we got married—in those days it was considered whorish to have carnal experience before marriage, even if you were in love. Paul's mother Dorothy also expected perfection in this, and I think she appreciated my chastity. It wasn't a secret.

The reception would go on, but it was time for the bride and groom to leave. As the guests waved a cheerful good-by, Paul and I drove away from our wedding reception in our beautifully painted MG— the car that had gone over the cliff. His middle finger was waving at the photographer who had insisted on taking formal shots. She didn't honor our instructions to capture the moments one by one, and dragged us around to create agonizing posed shots. While we ended up with a beautiful set of photos, we lost much precious reception time.

Paul and I left our wedding reception before the festivities ended, and at his request, but later we heard tales of family and friends partying for two days on Holden Road where I'd grown up. One of our neighbors, who enjoyed the alcoholic beverages at the wedding, was pulled out of the shrubs the next day, with leaf marks on his face.

Everyone seemed joyful on our wedding day. Even Paul's father Fred had kept his promise to be nice.

CHAPTER SIXTEEN

Marriage

Our honeymoon was not the best. When we arrived at the Pelham House on Cape Cod, Paul was ready, but I wasn't. His previous experience was irrelevant. He acted like a kid in a candy store and used a mechanical engineering approach to complete the task. We were like two bumbling neophytes. He tried everything but romance, and when it was over I wasn't sure it had even happened.

The next day I bought some ointment—a topical anesthetic— to alleviate the after effects of the previous night's activities. You'd think a nurse would know better; Paul was completely incapacitated. It took us a week to figure out why our first days of marriage were less than gratifying. It was a sad state of affairs.

During the following weeks, Paul learned the power of romance, and everything straightened out—pun intended.

We had only been married for two weeks when we flew out from Boston to Long Beach, California. We hated leaving our friends, the Goldbergs and the Dands, and my family, but I was excited about where life would take us.

When we arrived in Long Beach, we found a hotel for one night before moving into an apartment infested with cockroaches; within days we were living in a reasonable one-bedroom apartment. Our wedding gifts had gotten lost on their journey from the east coast, and we hadn't yet rented furniture, so we were living with virtually nothing. We had a pull-down bed with no sheets and a mattress pad for a blanket. We didn't want to buy anything because we knew supplies were coming.

A few days later, I got a job as a nurse in the operating room at Saint Mary's Hospital in Long Beach. I'd been working on the east coast, so it was easy to get the new position. The hospitals in Boston were known to be topnotch and looked great on the resume.

Paul had spent only a couple of nights with me before having to go out to sea trials up and down the coast of California. For many women, being alone was *not* a big deal, but where I came from, it was considered *heresy*.

Our apartment wasn't in the safest neighborhood in town. At first I felt uneasy sleeping in an apartment with only a single, simple lock between me and the street. But then I felt a surge of independence. I rose to my new life with ease until things on the streets of Long Beach started to percolate, and when the riots broke out in Watts, I took notice.

I knew that the situation was complex and a result of years of discrimination, but I wished to distance myself from the violence. We lived on First Street; the rioters were on Fourteenth.

When Paul came home for a couple of days from his maneuvers at sea, he introduced me to Joe and his wife Kathy. Paul and Joe worked together on the ship and the couple lived nearby.

It was decided that we wives would stay together during the following few days while our husbands were at sea, and they instructed us to go to the Navy Base if the riots got too dangerous. The couple's apartment was even closer to the problem than ours, so we decided that it would be best for Kathy to stay with me. Our wedding gifts had arrived, so we now had sheets, blankets, toasters, and all of the other staples we needed to function.

On our first and only night together, Kathy put a loaded gun on the nightstand next to the bed. I'd never seen a loaded gun, and found myself more intimidated by the gun being within inches of me than of the potential danger of rioters coming into our apartment in the middle of the night.

As the two of us sat riveted in front of the television, a newscaster ranted on about the chaos in Watts. [2] In Boston, news was presented in a perfunctory fashion, but this was different. The sensationalistic quality of the way the reporter went on about what was happening induced fear. "Rioters are out of control on Fourteenth Street," the newscaster announced with animation and drama. "They're burning and looting businesses and some are armed."

"If anyone comes, we have protection," Kathy announced confidently. She took her responsibility relative to the gun seriously. She also seemed balanced about the civil rights crisis, and I liked that she didn't seem prejudiced.

As the night went on, I found increased comfort in having a loaded weapon. Only ten minutes had passed when the newscaster updated his report, and new bulletins came within moments of each other for the next hour. Each felt more troubling than the one before, and each brought the violence closer to us on First Street.

When footage of burning buildings and angry rioters appeared, Kathy and I seriously considered our husbands' suggestion to go to the Navy base. The violence was advancing toward us and we could hear police sirens nearby. But the reporter on television said that people needed to lock their doors and stay inside, so we did.

By morning, the authorities reported that the police had secured control. It had been a long night, and I had to go to work. The hospital was located in the area of the riots. As I drove up the street I could see evidence of police and the National Guard on various corners and around the hospital.

The doctors and nurses in the operating room carried on in their usual fashion, with little discussion of what was happening. As medical people, we were there to take care of people and to do our jobs; politics were irrelevant to us while we were within the walls of the hospital.

---

2 The riots took place in the Watts neighborhood of Los Angeles, August 11-17, 1965.

Some people came to work late that day; a black orderly came in shaking. He said that on his way to work he'd been grabbed by the police, put up against a building, frisked, and that his bagged lunch had been confiscated and thrown in the trash. We bought him lunch and assured him that everything would be fine, and hoped that we were right.

Things did settle down in Watts, but in the aftermath things were still tense. I thought a party might be a good thing, so I invited the doctors, nurses, and other staff from the OR to come for a Friday night soiree. I wanted Paul to meet some of the people I worked with, and we were all ready for some fun.

About twenty people accepted the invitation, and all were young, but for one of the surgeons. Paul bought a keg of beer and put it in the bathtub with ice; by the time the beer was gone people were jumping into the swimming pool fully clothed and yelling like cowboys. One gay guy was hugging another and singing him Frank Sinatra's "Luck be a Lady" at the top of his lungs.

As the noise escalated, the manager arrived and threatened to evict us, but the party wouldn't stop. I had no influence on this group of raging fools, and the next day Paul and I were served with an eviction notice. "You have two weeks to get out," the manager announced.

The eviction actually came at a good time. Paul was told on the same day that he was being transferred to San Diego to start air traffic control school, and that we had to move.

I gave two week's notice, and during that last week at Saint Mary's, I started vomiting. When a nun asked me to assist in a radioactive implant, I requested that she send someone else in to scrub; I'd misplaced my birth control pills for a week, and I wasn't sure about my condition. If I was pregnant I wanted the baby to be healthy.

The move to San Diego was difficult. I felt too sick to lift my head from the pillow, but managed to drag myself out of bed to help Paul pack up our belongings. He organized them neatly in the back of the van that we'd bought with our wedding money and by two o'clock, we were ready to go.

We arrived in San Diego at dinnertime. Paul pulled into a drive-in Chinese restaurant and he ate egg rolls and pan-fried noodles while I hung my head out the window in misery as waves of intractable nausea came over me.

It was too late to go apartment hunting that night, so we got a hotel room and were in bed by ten. Sleep didn't always come, but when it did, it was my dearest friend. When I was sleeping, I wasn't gagging or throwing up; after only a few weeks of marriage, I had inadvertently become pregnant.

The next morning we got into the van and drove around looking for our next home. We were lucky to find an apartment near San Diego State College, and were offered reduced rent if we agreed to maintain the swimming pool, keep an eye on the tenants (mostly students), and collect rent—a great deal for us.

Paul was at school every day during the week, and between learning how to keep airplanes from crashing into each other and the rowdy tenants (those students loved to drink), he soon became exhausted.

In 1965 most men used the "F" bomb frequently and with great gusto, but rarely in front of women. But California was ahead of the curve in this regard. At night the parties were loud and we could hear the participants using it freely in every other sentence.

When Paul yelled out, "Don't swear in front of my wife," to the boys on the second floor, they responded with a chorus of, "Fuck you!" as chairs and boxes of soap powder were being hurled into the swimming pool from the balcony above and Bob Dylan's "The Times, They Are a Changin'," blared in the background.

Paul's own drunken college days had come back on him only a few months after his graduation.

Now and again I had a good day after the first trimester of the pregnancy. One night when I was about five months along, we'd been to the movies and had seen the great pie fight in *It's a Mad, Mad, Mad, Mad World* with Ethel Merman, Milton Berle, Sid Caesar, and other notables.

On the way home, Paul carried on with animation about the great pie fight. As he talked, I strategized. *I'm going to do it,* I thought gleefully. *Yes, I'm going to do it.*

When we got home, I slipped into the kitchen and subtly retrieved a lemon meringue pie from the fridge. As Paul came around the corner into the kitchen—*Bang!* I hit him square in the face with the pie. What transpired then was not pretty. I hid in the bathroom for an hour and finally realized it was futile. When I opened the door, he slathered me with the lemon meringue as we both laughed uncontrollably. A shower for both of us was the only answer.

Paul finished his training in San Diego. Within a few days of receiving his orders in December of 1965, we flew to San Francisco. Paul shipped out to Vietnam to serve as an engineering officer and air traffic controller. My poor husband spent Christmas Eve alone in Guam, after having eight immunizations in his arms the day before.

The baby was kicking in my belly as I walked up and down the hills of San Francisco on Christmas Day. Paul's sister Susan had been working as an intern in Oregon, and took the bus down so that we could both make the best of the holiday. My sadness was palpable and it was a rather dismal day for both of us.

After Christmas I went back to my parents' house for several months.

CHAPTER SEVENTEEN

Motherhood

In Paul's absence I'd been doing pretty much *nothing* except growing the baby. I slept in my old bedroom on Holden Road in Braintree, Massachusetts and waited. The aching in my heart for Paul was exacerbated by the intractable boredom that consumed me day after day. If it hadn't been for our close friends the Goldbergs taking me out once in awhile, I think I would have gone mad.

During the day everyone worked and I was often without a car. Sometimes, though, my parents let me have theirs. My mother worked at *Anne Starr*—a small, high-end clothing store—and I'd drop her off in the morning and pick her up at the end of the day. She always dressed with style and carried herself with dignity— and she sold a *lot* of expensive dresses. My father would take the bus to work and I'd pick him up at the shipyard.

I'd drive over to Paul's parent's house and visit his sweet mother who lived within minutes of us. Somehow I felt closer to Paul when I was with his mother, and I learned much about the family's history in the many hours I spent with her. While I was interested in what she had to say, she always looked back nostalgically rather than forward, and she spent more than an hour each morning on the phone commiserating with her widowed sister Marian who was ten years her senior.

At this time in my life I hadn't yet had an original thought. Spending so much time with Paul's mother—who had even fewer thoughts—was *not* a good thing.

On the morning of May 10, 1966, I woke up with intermittent back pain. My father, who realized I *might* be in labor, had to take the bus to work at 5:30 AM as his employer didn't allow time off for such things. My mother took the day off, and my mother-in-law came over and drove my mother and me to the hospital, leaving our car for my father to drive to the hospital after work.

Within a couple of hours I was wheeled down the hospital corridor toward the delivery room with my mother Dorothy on one side and my mother-in-law Dorothy on the other. Both were looking at me as if I might die at any moment. While I appreciated the support, I wanted to do this on my own, and they wouldn't have been allowed to be with me in the delivery room, anyway.

I had taken lessons in self-hypnosis for about a month. The anesthesiologist, Dr. Simon, would take care of me during the delivery, and I was ready. The guided imagery brought me to a totally relaxed state so I mentally could leave my body—*and* the pain—until I was ready to push the baby out.

Four doctors and three nurses observed Dr. Simon and me, waiting intently for the sight of the baby's head. The seven sets of eyes and serious faces stared down until the baby's head could be seen under a transparent amniotic sack that had not yet broken—no privacy here.

"Look! Her water never broke, and she's ready to deliver," the obstetrician said.

As the group bent in closer, amniotic fluid shot out with the velocity of a fire hose, hitting most of them in their faces and soaking their hair and clothing. They all broke out in laughter, and quickly dispensed towels to dry themselves. As the doctor wiped his brow he said, "I've never experienced anything like this in the thirty years I've been delivering babies."

Within minutes, the baby was born—three weeks early—so Paul missed the event. The umbilical cord was wrapped around her neck. Dr. Slomcowski removed it, and then lifted our baby girl up so I could see her clearly. She had every finger and every toe, and I was so relieved she didn't inherit Uncle Mario's nose.

Dr. Slomcowski placed her on my belly, and I could feel her little presence. It was magic. I snuck my arm down through the sheets until I felt the heat of her little back as it rose up and down. With our first touch, the weight of my loneliness lifted. This baby looked just like her father, and she filled the hole in my heart that had been left in his absence.

Paul and I had decided to name a baby boy, Christopher Paul or a baby girl, Lisa, but had been arguing about a girl's middle name in our letters for months during his deployment. I sent lists, but no names appealed to him. Finally, we agreed. Both our mothers were named Dorothy—a beautiful name, but it didn't seem to fit well with Lisa. So, we chose Joy—Lisa Joy Pimentel.

Paul learned of the birth of our daughter Lisa as he stood on the deck of the small destroyer rocking back and forth on the South China Sea. The jubilant news had relieved him of the endless hours of boredom, and also the periodic terror inflicted by attacks from the shore. He could hardly imagine he had a daughter.

During my three-day hospital stay, everyone felt sorry for me. A steady parade of my Italian relatives came through, and when I saw Aunt Cookie (my father's sister Egla) coming up the walkway with my mother-in-law Dorothy, I held my breath. Dorothy was dignified and very provincial; Cookie had a huge heart, but was tough and had few social graces. It wasn't unusual for her to flaunt her long legs and talk about how beautiful they were.

The nurses told the entourage they had to leave my room, and the last day in the hospital was the only peace I'd had since Lisa's birth.

Because my parents' house was so small, I'd prepared the crib so I could easily move to Paul's parents' house on his return. While I appreciated Paul's family, living with Paul's father was a challenge.

When Paul's ship arrived in Long Beach from Vietnam for the first time, he immediately hopped a plane to Boston. When I heard a vehicle pass the house, I thought a cab had moved too far down the street. Spotting a man in a white uniform in the distance, I ran for him. But it was just the ice cream man.

An hour later, a cab pulled up and Paul emerged. He hadn't changed much—he was still my handsome husband, but now the father of three-week-old Lisa.

I wanted to be alone with my husband and our new daughter, but that was not an option. Paul's parents and sister Susan allowed me to greet Paul alone, and even his father Fred tried to give us a little time. But when we went to bed, I felt ears on the bedroom door. While it could have been my imagination, I heard chuckling once and was embarrassed by the lack of privacy.

We stayed with Fred and Dorothy during Paul's two-week leave, and then we moved back to California. Paul returned to the ship off the coast of Long Beach. We secured a small apartment in San Pedro. Most of our neighbors were enlisted families; my husband was an officer. It was taboo for enlisted wives to fraternize with the wives of officers, and that made it a very lonely existence for me.

Before coming to California Paul and I had only visited places near our home in Massachusetts where we'd grown up and been educated. The farthest our travels had taken us was to the World's Fair in New York City; Paul refused to wait in lines, so we'd seen nothing. Coming to California was a huge adventure for us.

While in San Pedro, Paul was on the ship much of the time testing weapons and gear in preparation for his second deployment, so I found myself alone—a lot.

During Paul's absence I had only two visitors. Paul's sisters Joanie and Susan stayed for a couple of weeks, and later my brother Dick stopped on his way through California. He'd come with four young, enthusiastic Marines who were eager to "go and fight the communists." Their stay wasn't fun—they all got sick with fevers and coughs. So I fed them soup, and when they felt better, they were on their way.

A week after the Marines left with my brother, our nine-month-old baby Lisa became very ill and could barely breathe. Lisa's little chest pulled in and out, and she was gasping for breath.

In the dead of night I realized we were both burning with fever and needed help. Lisa's fever was 104 degrees and mine was 103. Panic struck when I tried to call an ambulance and our telephone failed.

At first I knocked on a door across the hall. When there was no response, I left Lisa and ran desperately to other apartments that faced the parking lot of the housing development, and literally *pounded* on the doors of strangers in search of help. My knuckles were bruised and swollen, but nobody answered. Perhaps their husbands were also out to sea, and they were afraid.

As I ran back to our apartment, I grabbed the baby and put her into her basket on the back seat of the car—no car seats *then*. With every breath, Lisa was straining for air.

San Pedro stood high above Long Beach, and as I drove I had no idea where I was going. The fever made it difficult for me to think clearly, but then I remembered the small military hospital at the bottom of the hill.

When I arrived, it took only moments for a young doctor to grab Lisa out of my arms and take her to the treatment room. Nurses put a tiny oxygen tube into her nose, but even so, she could barely cry for lack of air.

My baby's throat was scarlet and her larynx was swollen almost shut. Within a half hour, she was full of antibiotics and steroids. The doctor then carried her to a hospital room and placed her in a crib with an oxygen tent. He opened a tracheotomy kit and kept it on a table next to him; if the swelling became even the slightest bit worse, he would have had to cut into her trachea to get air into her lungs. The doctor then sat on a chair next to the crib and waited—and waited some more.

"Why did you wait so long?" the doctor asked, in an accent typical of the Philippines.

"I'm so sorry," I told him in an almost dazed state. "We've both been sick since yesterday, and she just took a turn—I wish I'd come sooner."

As I stood listlessly next to the crib, *I* continued to burn with fever. The doctor had no idea of it. I drank several glasses of water during the course of the night hoping that it would help.

The following morning, I broke into a sweat—and suddenly—*my* fever was gone. I was exhausted, but I had turned a corner.

The young Asian doctor had stayed at Lisa's crib for the entire night, and half of the next day. News of Lisa's illness had traveled through the military wives' grapevine and reached Paul's ship. The wife of the captain had paid a visit to the hospital staff—and specifically to the doctor—to let them know she expected excellence.

Lisa's 104° fever dropped to 102, and her breathing improved. The young doctor went home. I was grateful—so *very* grateful.

My daughter remained in the hospital for a week, having ups and downs for the first several days. More than once, I was terrified that she would die. She kept crying and reaching for me, but they'd told me to leave her in the oxygen tent.

When I couldn't stand her crying anymore, I picked her up and held her close to me. We both calmed as she laid her head next to my heart. The nurse had set a rocking chair next to the crib—perfect.

As the week went on, Lisa's face gave evidence of the steroids she'd been given to reduce the inflammation in her throat. She was very round, but she was ready to come home.

When Lisa was discharged, the doctor told me she'd contracted a nasty streptococcus infection. I felt the coldness in his voice. I knew he was mad at me for waiting so long to bring my baby to him. I felt terribly about that. The doctor and I had never really connected. Perhaps he resented the fact that the captain's wife had been there; I hadn't asked her to intervene, but I was happy she had.

During Lisa's illness I realized what it meant to be a mother, and how difficult it was to be a Navy wife. Paul wasn't home; it seemed he was *never* home. We later determined that we'd been together for a total of about three *months* during his three-*year* stint in the Navy. I vowed to never have another child; I was sure I was incapable. I wondered if I had the strength to be alone in circumstances such as these, but I had no choice—I had a daughter.

In the spring of 1967, when Paul was in Vietnam for the second time, I went back to Braintree for a few months. The neighbors in California had continued to be distant and I wanted familiar people around me.

We celebrated Lisa's first birthday a week after arriving in Boston. My father, in his usual fashion, had planned a fun party. When I arrived, he pointed to a whimsical 6-foot manikin that resembled the scare crow from "The Wizard of Oz" and said, "We invited Paul to Lisa's party." We had the usual parade, and food, and I was happy I'd come home.

The next week my father set up a contest. My uncles took close-up pictures of their noses which my father then sent to the sailors on Paul's ship, asking them to decide which nose was biggest. None were *small*, but some *were* bigger than others. The Pasquale brothers were proud of their Italian noses, and never hesitated to flaunt them.

Uncle Mario, winner of the International Nose Contest on Paul's ship

Apparently the wives' tale that relates to large noses is true. In the end, Uncle Mario (who was called "Rigatoni" on occasion by his wife and brothers) won the grand prize.

I moved back to California in the fall hoping the birth of our second baby would coincide with the end of Paul's second tour of duty. We knew it would be close.

As it turned out, I was standing on the pier with an enormous belly when his ship arrived in Long Beach—the baby was late. My body was thin but my belly stuck out so far that people would chuckle when I walked by. When Paul spotted me from the ship as it pulled into the dock, he laughed, too.

The day after our son Christopher was born in November, they sent me home, and the following day Paul returned to the ship. His sister Joanie had come to help me on the first day I was home, but after that, I was alone with a new baby and a seventeen-month-old. It was difficult. I was also exhausted and depressed.

By the time Christopher was a few months old, he was chuckling aloud often, and Lisa adored him. He was a good-natured baby, but he was hungry—all the time—day and night. While I didn't get much sleep it was great to be able to eat as much as I wanted and stay really thin.

We considered ourselves fortunate to have calm and happy babies, delighted to have a son and a daughter.

CHAPTER EIGHTEEN

Dickie

In March of 1968, my little brother Dick was discharged from the Marines after spending thirteen months in Vietnam. Dick had spent his tour of duty gathering intelligence in the secret corners of North Vietnam—an extremely dangerous assignment; many Recon Marines never made it home.

I was surprised and relieved when he stopped by our apartment on his way back to Massachusetts. When I opened the door of our small California apartment, I found my brother staring at me like a statue. I was stunned; it was difficult to believe he was finally home and safe.

Dick wasn't a tall man, but his shoulders were wide, and he'd always been very strong and solidly built. As he stood in the darkness of the hallway, the musty dampness of the jungle emanated from his uniform, and I could see that he'd lost most of his hair.

I pulled him into the apartment, and hugged him tightly. His response was almost robotic. His skin had a yellow tint. He had contracted malaria during his tour, and the remnants of illness showed on his face.

"Let's call Mom and Dad, Dick. They need to know you're here and that you're OK." It was three hours later on the east coast—and after midnight—but we agreed that it would be best to call them, anyway.

My mother's faith in Jesus had kept her together for the year that my brother had been away, but her worst fear had been that

Dick would die in his last days in the jungle. It was common for the dead and wounded to be shown on television, and my mother Dorothy spent hours in front of the TV hoping to see my brother alive and well. At one point she'd been sure she'd seen him transporting a wounded soldier on a stretcher during the 6 o'clock news; television did *not* hold back the images in 1967 or the details of the sites of the battles.

We knew Dickie had been in many intense "situations"—and had witnessed *horrible* things. Believing she'd seen him well and together was reassuring for my mother.

So, when the phone rang in the middle of the night, my parents didn't answer it quickly. It was likely my father held his breath before picking up the receiver, my mother standing next to him terrified.

At first Dick thought the call didn't go through. "Hello, Mom and Dad—it's Dick."

Only silence.

"It's Dick," he repeated. "I'm at Sandra's in California."

He then heard the sobs.

"I'm OK. I'll see you tomorrow."

My brother showed no emotion during the call. He seemed almost perfunctory, as if he could've been calling after spending a day at the ball game. I wondered if this transition was too much for him to absorb; twenty-four hours earlier he'd been in the thick of it in Southeast Asia.

When the call was over I offered my brother something to eat.

"No thanks, San, I'm not hungry."

"Well, we'll have tea, then," I replied.

I boiled a pan of water, and put two cups on the table with a few chocolate chip cookies. I knew he wouldn't be able to resist them; as kids my brother and I would eat an entire bag of cookies at one sitting. We'd often had tea together when we were growing up; the scene was familiar to both of us.

Over the cup of tea, he talked and I listened.

As the night went on, he talked about averting ambush after ambush, and sleeping in the jungle of North Vietnam for weeks without being able to breathe freely at night—for fear of being heard—and subsequently killed.

Dick talked about having been chased for days, escaping close calls. He elaborated on a particular experience, and as I listened, I realized my little brother had become a warrior.

"I always forced my squad to carry their fifty-pound backpacks through alternate routes of thick jungle, so we could see the enemy waiting for us on the beaten paths below. My men hated *it*—and *me*—then, but when they saw the first ambush waiting for them, they knew why I'd made 'em do it."

He paused and went on without intensity. "Once we were completely surrounded, and in the center of the ambush there was a hill—I thought it was the end for us."

"What did you do?"

"It was a crap shoot and the odds were *not* good. We played them anyway; we had *nothing* to lose; I decided if I could get to the top of the hill alive, I might be able to divert the North Vietnamese soldiers away from the squad, and create an escape route. I scaled the hill with my rifle, several clips, and three grenades. One of my men came with me, armed and ready.

"I'd told the squad to wait until we ran out of ammunition before opening fire. We reached the crest and crouched down with our ammunition ready next to us.

"Before I fired the first round, I vowed that, *if I survived*, I'd have everything and anything I *wanted* in life."

I found this a curious vow to make at such a trying time.

Dick and his partner blasted rounds into the thick jungle below, and tossed their grenades in succession, giving the impression that there were many soldiers.

My brother had been the kind of child who wouldn't leave my mother's side, and at night he would crawl into my parents' bed at the first rumble of thunder. It was difficult to imagine him in such a situation.

When Dick and his fellow Marine had tossed their last grenade from the top of the hill, his men opened fire from their lower position.

At that point the North Vietnamese soldiers believed that *they* were the ones who would soon be surrounded if they didn't retreat around the hill, so they left swiftly. This opened up an escape route for Dick and his men.

"Then what?"

"It took us a day to trek back over the border to our base in South Vietnam, but we made it back."

"Wow, that's amazing, really amazing. How're you feeling now Dick, you doing OK?"

"I'm OK, I'm getting better, but the malaria was a really bad thing." He looked toward the window and into the darkness as he went on. "While I was in the hospital, all my men were killed in an ambush."

"Oh my God, I'm so sorry. You had so many near-death experiences with these guys—it must be terrible for you."

He just continued looking out the window—he said nothing and showed no emotion. But, it was then I knew he'd had his sweet sleep taken away forever.

"You did your very best Dick, you didn't ask to get malaria, it just happened. This is awful, and it'll take time. I wish I knew how to make it feel better for you—you deserve to be happy."

My brother shrugged and didn't reply. This was not the brother I knew who would *never* have missed an opportunity to talk.

At that point I asked him about the young men who'd visited our apartment thirteen months earlier. "How did Plunkett and the other three guys do?" I asked.

"None of them made it," Dick answered soberly. I felt sick to my stomach, and wished I hadn't asked the question.

Then Dick asked me about the demonstrators and called them *traitors*. I thought about it for a minute and said, "It's hard to see now Dick, but in a way you were in Vietnam so that they could be free to protest. Democracy doesn't always feel fair."

He didn't respond.

My brother left for Braintree early the next morning. Unlike many of his friends, Dick would be welcomed home with gratitude and love.

My parents still lived on Holden Road in the house where we'd lived with Grandma Bessie and then Uncle Geoff. The entire dead end street was filled with friends and relatives from the *Point* and with the neighbors who'd put a huge banner across the road that said, "Welcome Home."

The press was there to get his story, and when they asked Dick about the war protesters, he replied, "That's why I fought." There was no mention in his interview about the horror he'd experienced.

Dick was a very good man, but after his experience in Vietnam he kept running. His jovial facade became almost frenetic, and he never came up for air.

My brother went on with his life. He married his high school sweetheart and lived his life with her and their three children with little mention of the war.

He didn't collect weapons, or try to seal his pain with substances, but the gun he kept tucked under his bed every night was a reflection of his life in the jungle. His sense of vigilance remained heightened. The people in the next town became "the potential enemy" who could come in and hurt his family at any time.

In our childhood, my brother had been a sweet and gentle little boy and when he grew I was in awe of him. He was a superb athlete and a state gymnastics champion—the kind of man who could do almost anything he wanted to do, but he was a casualty of war both physically and mentally. He mastered many careers and his diverse skills allowed him to keep the promise he'd made to himself during the battle on the hilltop in Vietnam—"I will have anything and everything I want."

When he came close to his financial edge, he always figured out a way to survive in style with his dignity intact.

Though he acquired beautiful houses, it didn't take him long to tire of one, then move to another. He had the best of everything, and seemed to be trying to fill the emptiness with *stuff*.

Dick was a very *funny* man. He had a gift for making people laugh, but just under the surface were the tears he'd never shed, and the continuous drive to be and do everything.

He bought a Martin guitar and—in a matter of weeks—learned to play classical flamenco music. He became an amazing magician, levitating people in his living room, baffling crowds. At one point he was a jeweler who bought his wife diamonds and gold, a teacher of electronics, and a professional pool player—all at the same time. In his later years, he got his real estate license, and successfully sold houses.

In his late fifties my brother's body began to weaken, and he became ashen and winded. During a summer visit I suggested that his illness could be a consequence of Agent Orange, or the malaria he had contracted during the war, but he wouldn't entertain the thought. As a Marine his first duty was to protect the United States of America and in his mind, it would have been treason to blame the country for his medical condition. Marines couldn't question; *he* couldn't question.

We both knew he was sick. He'd been making plans during the previous months, and told me about what he wanted in the event of his death. He'd been diagnosed with pneumonia in a Florida hospital. I suspected worse as he was scheduled for a biopsy. When he called me from that emergency room, I could feel his fear. "My lungs are really screwed up, San. I can't get enough air."

I booked a flight from Boston to Florida, but by the time I arrived, he was in an induced coma, and by the next day his face and head had become distorted and unrecognizable. As his daughter Michelle and I stood by his side, he slipped away.

My greatest sadness was that my brother had convinced all those around him of his success, while never having convinced himself. His magic tricks, houses, jewelry, cars, and the classical music he played on his Martin guitar couldn't fill the hole that had been left in his heart during the war. When Dickie died, all the material things that had been important to him dissipated, leaving only the legacy of a hero.

Richard Panfilio Pasquale

CHAPTER NINETEEN

At Last

Paul had called me once from Japan (just before the end of his second tour in Vietnam in the fall of 1967) to tell me that they would send him to Rhode Island if he signed up for another four years, and when I started sobbing he knew it wasn't going to happen.

When Paul was discharged from the Navy, I breathed a sigh of relief and he accepted a job in Albion, Michigan as an engineer. He'd been wined and dined into thinking it was the best place in the universe. While I was hoping to go home to Braintree, he wanted to take the job. As it wasn't in Southeast Asia, I rolled over.

PART 2

CHAPTER TWENTY

Family and Community Life

As we approached our new town, the bright orange letters of the large *Sunshine Inn and Restaurant* sign—the only structure in an asphalt parking lot—loomed in the distance.

I was tired when we were assigned a room on the first floor. My third pregnancy had taken the spunk out of me. The night manager, who was the first of many really nice mid-westerners we met, took us to our room and helped set up a crib for Chris and a cot for Lisa, and wished us the best.

More than two-thirds of all housing in Albion had been built prior to 1940, and it was difficult to find any place to live in this small city of 12,000 people. High employment in the feeder industries created the housing shortage. Every day I'd call real estate agencies from our motel room in hope of finding a place— any place—but weeks, and then months, passed without any options.

At first I loved not having to worry about cooking or cleaning, and that the company was paying all our expenses while at the inn. But after eating mediocre food from a mediocre menu for several weeks, the novelty wore off. When a mouse ran across the floor of our motel room, I was *spent*.

Finally the bank called—three months later in the spring! "We have a house for you," the banker said, "but you can't go inside because of legal issues with the owners."

"Well, if we can't see it, what should we do?" I asked.

"I suggest you drive by and give us a call if you like it—it's a rare opportunity and a foreclosure."

"I'll go now," I replied.

I called Paul, settled the babies in the car, and drove to the other side of town to see the house.

As I drove up the street it became clear that the bank agent was not exaggerating when he described it as "the most sought-after street in town." Each house stood on a large lot and the owners clearly took pride in their property. The stately house on the corner impressed me and appeared to be in good condition. After living in one room at the *Sunshine Inn* for three months with two babies, I was ready.

In the two years before Paul and I had married, I'd managed to save enough to buy a piece of land in Massachusetts from my Uncle Geoffrey as an investment and it turned out to be a very good thing.

We sold the land and between that money and a small loan from Paul's father, we cobbled together the down payment. We bought that first house for $11,000 without ever seeing the inside.

The house was *not* what it had appeared to be as we drove by. It was, in fact, a dump *with potential*. The ceilings were covered with wallpaper. The walls, cabinets, hinges, and woodwork in the kitchen were navy blue, and the solid oak floors had accumulated layers and layers of wax and varnish over the years. The house was dark and gloomy, and I felt negative energy in every room.

Paul reassured me that we could make it a *palace*—such is the nature of young optimism.

When fall came the crisp air smelled like breakfast toast and the majestic oak and maple trees in our yard manifested luxurious shades of red and orange. I always found time for the children and me to be outside.

Lisa and Chris ran into huge piles of leaves on the lawn, making the work of raking almost impossible, but I didn't care. Being away from the dingy walls and navy blue kitchen was a gift.

Paul's job required him to be working much of the time, but on weekends we always enjoyed a big breakfast with our children, and Paul and I often enjoyed some time chatting while our kids played after the meal.

On a particular Saturday morning in 1968 as Lisa and Chris were amusing themselves in the dining room after breakfast, Paul read a newspaper article about the Vietnam War.

As a young man, Paul's dream had been to join the Navy. He viewed himself a nimble seaman. During his adolescence he'd become the lead crewman on a racing boat, and the excitement and challenge of the ocean had captured his imagination. When he graduated from ROTC at Harvard he was excited that he could represent his country while doing something he loved to do. The war in Vietnam hadn't been in the forefront of his thinking—the opportunity to drive a ship was all-consuming. We'd started our lives in the aftermath of the Eisenhower years when people believed "America could do no wrong," and we'd been caught up in a nationalistic coma that kept us asleep for the first two decades of our lives.

As a "no nonsense" engineer, often Paul had been unaware of *what* he was feeling or *why*. But, reading the article that morning brought back memories of an event from his days in the Navy two years before, and with them, a new awareness.

It was 1966 and Paul's ship was moving through the South China Sea when a little old Vietnamese man wearing a hemp belt and a traditional broad brimmed hat appeared in front of them. His sampan was rocking up and down next to Paul's ship. The poor soul was screaming loudly in his native language and gesturing for the ship to move away.

Paul was a young lieutenant and the officer of the deck that day[3], which meant he was driving the ship when he'd inadvertently dragged it over the man's fishing net, demolishing it.

---

3   A naval officer responsible for the operation of the ship in the absence of the captain or the executive officer. Abbreviation: O.O.D.

The infuriated fisherman responded by brandishing an old single-shot rifle and began shooting deliberately but erratically at the ship. It took him only seconds to reload and fire again—and yet again.

Paul ordered warning shots to be fired from the 30-caliber machine gun mounted on the deck behind him. A double spray of bullets splashed in the water in front of the sampan, but it didn't deter the man's furor; he continued to aim at the steel sides of the large destroyer, and the bullets bounced off like popcorn.

Paul was certain that the fisherman was simply a fisherman, but it didn't matter—he called general quarters in order to clear the deck and protect his men, while hoping that the man would come to his senses. He didn't.

The machine of war took over; the massive guns turned until they were pointed straight at the fisherman as he continued his angry outcry.

The die had been cast, and war is war; the captain took over and gave the order. In an instant the little man and his sampan had been blown into tiny pieces of flesh, blood, wood, and bones. The only remnant of the man's long existence was his damaged hat gently bobbing on the open ocean.

Images of the little old man with the conical straw hat had been hidden in the remote recesses of Paul's mind since he'd left Southeast Asia. But on this day questions began to percolate, and the wall of denial that had served him so well for so long fell away.

Paul looked at me and asked, "Why didn't I just turn away? I *could* have—I *should* have.

My belly was bulging in its eighth month. The only available doctor in town who could deliver my third baby was the obstetrician Dr. Banger, inspiring any number of jokes from Paul.

We'd completed painting and putting a new ceiling in the baby's room by the time Susan was born. She was our only planned baby, and we didn't have any gender preference, since we already had both a girl and a boy.

I know that when women talk about their childbirth experiences, it can be colossally boring and most of us talk as if we're the only ones to have ever experienced it. But, bearing a child is the *sixth* most common cause of death among women between the ages of 20-34 in the United States.[4]

I apologize in advance for the elaboration. But, it's one small, God-damned hole for such a package.

Lisa and Chris had been born in "state of the art" medical facilities. Albion was a small and remote location, and I wasn't confident about the quality of care available. I was concerned for my baby and for myself, and actually thought about going to Boston for the delivery. But with two other children, going east wasn't an option. Dr. Banger seemed like a nice enough man and he had delivered hundreds of babies, so I let my concerns go.

The birth was very difficult; the "self hypnosis" I had used with my other two children was ineffective in light of what happened; when they induced me with *Pitocin*[5], the effects were immediate, and *very* intense. While labor is always painful, the contractions induced with medication were more powerful and frequent than any I'd ever experienced, and I was wheeled into the delivery room within minutes.

I couldn't stop myself from screaming from way down in my gut. It was as if I was another person, a woman I didn't recognize.

---

4   Article: The Disturbing Shameful History of Childhood Deaths: Laura Helmuth *Slate*'s science and health editor

5   Pitocin is used to induce labor.

I screamed and screamed without a break, as I felt my perineum tear.

By the time I heard Susan cry, I was torn apart from top to bottom, inside and out, and without anesthesia.

Paul seldom cried in our early years, but he cried on this day. In those times men weren't allowed in the room when their babies were born. When he heard my screaming and deep groaning cries from the waiting room, he cried with me. He later said, "I felt like I was listening to you being tortured."

They took my baby daughter Susan away without me seeing her, and I hadn't noticed because I was blind with pain as the doctor kept stitching and pulling the tissue together as I cried out. Unfortunately, the repair was complete by the time the local anesthetic took effect.

Dr. Banger wasn't cruel; things were just not as advanced in some places as others. It felt like the doctor was mending a big hole in a torn blanket. When he was finished, he left the delivery room with a swift goodbye. There were seldom apologies in those days—this was part of a normal day for many doctors and their patients. I was relieved that he was done with me, and committed (again) to never having another baby.

My mother had often told me what it was like for her when she gave birth to me, and now I understood. Her experience had been similar, but it took longer. She said they had also taken me away as soon as I was born.

I spent four days in the hospital after I gave birth, and didn't sit down for a week. That too was common for mothers back then.

When Susan was born, she and I were both robbed of the glory of it. I wish I could go back in time to do it differently; I would demand to hold her and insist that she stay with me.

Shortly after Susan's birth, Paul lost his enthusiasm for renovating the house. He continued to work fourteen-hour days.

I'd cook and clean the house, but it always felt dirty. I was disgusted when a mouse ran out from under a dishrag on the counter while I was making a pie. *At least we don't have rats*, I thought.

There were so many things wrong with the house, and they all aggravated me. The rusty discolored toilet in the upstairs bathroom bothered me the most. I'd have to rattle and shake the handle, take off the back lid, and put the bulb back where it belonged at every use—it was a colossal pain.

On one very hot day in July, I started to sweat as I sat on the rusty toilet seat. At first I thought it was the humidity of the day, but later I felt heat rising from the toilet bowl while dipping out the babies' diapers. Paul had hooked up a hot water pipe to it by mistake, and the scalding poop made me gag. As he'd been working on a water system at work that was as complicated as it was big, it was surprising that he could make such a mistake.

At the end of a cold winter's day I moved slowly up the stairs carrying Susan in my arms. When I spotted a huge rat in her room, I was furious. Later, I was flooded with emotions when I announced to Paul that I'd be moving back *home* to Massachusetts. He immediately dismissed the idea and told me I was being a hysteric.

"Where are you going to get the money to go home?" he asked. "I'll set up a trap and the rat will be gone—you're being ridiculous."

Several nights went by—the trap remained empty. I kept the baby in our bedroom at night and checked on the other kids several times during the night. I was constantly making sure the doors to their rooms were closed.

In the midst of nighttime drama with the rat, we had two tornado warnings. The local fire department blared a *very loud* siren incessantly to warn people that a tornado was nearby.

In the daytime the sky could turn black and sometimes funnel clouds appeared in the distance. Lightning raced across the sky until it found its place on earth, and thunder resounded. When daylight turned to night and a storm raged in the Midwest, it felt like Armageddon.

When the storms came at night, I'd wake everyone in the house, and take the kids to the dungeon-like basement. It was nothing less than creepy, and all I could think of was the rat.

On the first night Paul came with us and the tornado didn't touch down near us. On the second night when the alarm went off, I grabbed the baby, gathered the other kids, and headed downstairs to the basement in my usual fashion. Paul had barely stirred—"Don't worry about it honey, it'll be OK," he said half asleep. His complacency made me want to slap him. *Men are idiots*, I thought.

Paul wasn't alone. Most people in town slept through the warnings because of an old Indian tale; the story was that the fork in the river prevented tornados from hitting town. But I wouldn't buy it, there was too much at stake.

My children were half asleep as we sat on the stairs in the damp basement waiting for the final siren to release us. When I spotted the long black tail of the bastard rat sitting motionless behind a beam and realized it was dead, I should have been jubilant. But dead or alive, the rat petrified me.

It took me some time and thinking to settle down. I knew that our house had great potential. It was a good-sized two-story house built in the 1930s, with three bedrooms and a bath and a half. The tiny half bath was located in a small den off the dining room and both rooms were very dark and dingy. I also knew we didn't have the wherewithal to finish it quickly.

Because of Paul's work schedule, there was little time left to finish big projects at home. I finally accepted that it was going to be like this for a very long time, and I let it all go.

During the second year in the little city, I jumped into community life aggressively, and joined every organization that would have me. This was the first real community I had lived in since we'd been married, and I found it exciting to be part of the Welcome Wagon, The JC-ettes, and to teach Sunday School.

Paul was a member of the Junior Chamber of Commerce. I too wanted to support the community, but could only join the JC-ettes, the women's auxiliary to the Junior Chamber. I felt compelled to challenge their policy of not inviting women into the Chamber—a challenge not well-received.

The JC-ettes had sponsored a "Woman of the Year," competition, and I was nominated by another organization. When I won, an uncomfortable tension filled the room. Sour faces winced as the head of the organization presented me with the award.

My having stepped out of a designated female role, and possibly the article about me in the paper, may have incensed them even more. While I felt it was an honor to be chosen, the whole experience had a sort of sting to it. This would be the first of many uncomfortable moments in my new-found paradigm of liberalism.

Albion, as a whole, was experiencing challenging times. Those who saw it as a slow, peaceful farm community were unaware that it was "a small town glutted at its edges with heavy industry" populated by "people whose pace is rural and whose problems are urban."[6] Only forty-five minutes from Detroit, Albion was a microcosm of the large troubled city. Martin Luther King, Jr. had been assassinated and there was serious racial tension across the country. Albion had seen its own share of trouble in the halls of the high school, and people were concerned.

I had tried to convince Paul that children needed to be part of a religion to give them stability. He thought it was *bologna*, but in light of my aggravation about the condition of the house, he caved in. Though Paul was raised Catholic, he reluctantly attended the Episcopal Church with me.

One evening we attended a forum at our priest's house with representatives from the African American Baptist Church across town to address the *racial issues* that had been affecting the community.

---

6 "Albion: City That Confessed – And Then, Restitution Began;" *State Journal*, n.d.

We left the children with a babysitter, crossed the street, and knocked on Father Mark's door. He and his wife Ann greeted us, and we followed them into a small sitting room where eight chairs had been arranged in a circle. China teacups and a plate stacked high with homemade butter-laden pastries were neatly arranged on a small table.

Three black women sat next to one another. Their church was located on the other side of town and well away from the railroad tracks, the town's clear line of demarcation between blacks and whites. When the conversation started, all the chairs were occupied. There was an uneasy tension that sometimes happens when people first meet each other and a bit more because black and white people seldom socialized in that town. As the eight of us faced one another Father Mark's wife Ann began the dialogue.

"What can we do about these foolish kids who date each other?" she asked, in reference to inter-racial dating.

One of the black women squirmed in her seat and looked to the floor. "I don't know, but I've told my children not to do it."

While some people may have approved of interracial marriages in 1968, Gilda wasn't one of them.

Why aren't we talking about real *problems?* I thought.

Ann's question shouldn't have surprised me; interracial marriage was unpopular in America. In those days I could be self-righteous and surly when I thought something wasn't right. But being in our preacher's house tempered me. I had grown up in the church and had supported Richard Nixon for president in the early '60s, so thinking freely and expressing progressive values was not something I did easily.

"I guess I don't understand. What's the big deal about kids who don't look the same dating each other?" I asked.

There was silence and an uncomfortable moment when everyone was trying to determine what to do with my question. I could see Father Mark thinking as he moved his lanky legs back and forth. His forehead creased as his eyes squinted; he seemed uncomfortable. "You have a point . . . I think you have a point," he replied intently.

We were walking through a social minefield.

"It seems to me that some of these kids are rebelling against their parents, and the others—well—maybe they just like each other," I said.

Though I was twenty-six years old and religious, a slightly adolescent zeal came over me. I giggled in jest and said, "It seems that the kids should be meeting to figure out how to put up with *the likes* of us adults."

Ann replied quickly, "What if there are pregnancies, the poor children will grow up being picked on by both sides."

I said, "You're right, the kids will have challenges, but we shouldn't be among them. Don't you see that it all starts with us?" My tone was more condescending than it was arrogant, but I couldn't have been more self-righteous. The corners of Paul's mouth gently lifted. I knew he was enjoying my challenge.

Father Mark also challenged his wife's comments. He then asked an elder named Charlie, how he felt about interracial dating.

"I can't even think about it, it's too scary for a guy like me," he replied. Charlie had been brought up in Alabama at a time when a black man could be hung if someone thought he looked at a white woman the wrong way.

"Datin' wasn't thought about where I come from. But if I was to go to a store that sold Coke on the hottest day of the summer, they'd stare at me till I was gone, and if I evah asked for a Coke, well, let's just say I wouldn't." [7]

I'd heard about the Coke issue, but I'd never talked to anyone who'd experienced it.

Our attention then moved to the frail and soft-spoken African American church lady, Gilda, who was sitting next to me. She explained that she'd moved to Albion ten years earlier after having lived in Mississippi for most of her forty-five years.

When we asked her if she liked Albion she said it was "fine." She went on to say that when she lived in the south, she had to

---

7   http://www.theatlantic.com/health/archive/2013/01/why-we-took-cocaine-out-of-soda/272694/

get up every morning at six in time to catch the truck to go pick cotton.

I'd always thought that picking cotton was the plight of slavery; I didn't know that it hadn't ended there. Gilda said that sometimes her gloves would wear out, and her hands would be bleeding from the sharp tips of the bolls.

"By ten in the morning, my feet was blistering hot from the heat in the field, and my bladder was achin'—they was suppose to let us go to the bathroom, but they din't," Gilda explained.

While hearing the "N" word was like the sound of a fingernail scratching against a black board, this was what I heard next. The sweet little woman was somber when she told us that at the end of the day her boss would yell at the crew and say, "Niggas—get in the truck."

"Things are so much better in Albion, so much better, and I thank God every day for it," Gilda explained.

As Gilda looked down at her scarred and worn hands, she went on to say that she took care of her two boys at home until her husband became ill—they were still babies. It was then that she went to work in the fields. When her mother—and then her husband—died, it had been more difficult. There were days when they had no food, little income, and no childcare.

"The neighbors did what they could, but some was struggling more than me. Then God was so good to me, and my prayers got answered."

When her aunt in Albion learned her sister had died, she wanted to help Gilda and her children. People in her church helped bring Gilda and her boys to Albion.

After Gilda became established in Albion, she got a job as a cleaning attendant at the local hospital. While she continued to struggle financially, things improved when her kids were old enough to work. She wasn't happy that her oldest son quit school for a specific job, but found life easier with the additional income.

When Gilda was finished telling her story, I felt like a shallow and petty loser for complaining so much about my house on Irwin

Ave. I was left wondering if things had changed for the cotton pickers of Mississippi.

"It's hard for people like us to understand the breadth of your experience," I said, "I feel sad that your life was so hard, and angry that anyone would treat people so badly—it's shameful."

Gilda told me not to fret, and that her life was "pretty good" in Albion. She said she loved her church and her neighbors, and that she was happy.

While Gilda seemed content, she went on to say that her children were very mad about lots of things, and it was this that made her decide to come to the meeting. She explained that her boys were getting caught up with the way they thought things should be, because they were too young to remember Mississippi.

"My boys say that black people can't buy houses, and can't get good jobs, and that people assume they're stupid because they're not white. They don't seem to be able to be happy with the way things are."

Ann showed signs of discomfort with the dialogue, but jumped on the fact that Gilda didn't like that her boys were angry.

"Well it's really good that you recognize that they're being unnecessarily angry, but we're not going to solve anything more tonight," Ann said. "Let's take time to enjoy our tea before we say good-night."

Father Mark said, "Thanks for coming. It was interesting and important."

We enjoyed the refreshments and then the evening ended with gracious goodbyes. But, I'm not sure we did a thing to help the "youth situation" in town. Paul and I later determined that underneath it all, the African American participants didn't give a rat's ass about interracial dating, but were more invested in promoting harmony than making social commentary.

Paul had often talked about his "Catholic fraud." When he was a teen he went to confession, but he always left out the bad sins like fornication, in favor of admitting that he had taken God's name in vain.

He would often ramble on like an evangelist himself—"Look at King Henry the Eighth, the Crusades, Ireland, Israel and Palestine, and let us not forget the crooks that rant on in tents in order to get money from people who can't afford it.

"Then we have the charming Inquisition when people cut the heads off of anyone who disagreed with them, and through it all were pedophiles lurking in confessionals like foxes in chicken coops." Even *then* Paul had heard about the pedophiles.

There was nobody on earth more irreverent than my husband. He had always had definite ideas about religion, ideas I'd never even considered for fear of going to hell. I also worried about him going to hell, but told myself that God would never do such a thing to such a nice guy.

On the following Sunday after the meeting at Father Mark's, Paul and I took the kids to church. He wanted to appease me because of his long hours of work, and this was a way to spend time with us and make me happy.

Father Mark was friendly enough, but I knew he was feeling uncomfortable about what had happened at his house.

On this day, while repeating the words I'd been saying since I could talk, I was more mindful as we sat down, kneeled down, and got up again.

How bored God must be; every weekend he watches people kneeling and jumping up and down in church on His behalf for hours on end. I think He'd be much happier if we were nice to each other.

As a child I'd gone to church every Sunday—my mother insisted on it. Though my last name was Pasquale, my father had converted from Catholicism to become an Episcopalian. My mother was Methodist and deeply religious and the Episcopal Church felt like a good compromise for both of them.

While growing up I had often felt like a religious oxymoron. With a name like Pasquale, it was odd to be an Anglican; sometimes I felt like a highlander eating spaghetti, and other times, like a Roman with a bagpipe.

As Paul and I sat in the pew listening to the sermon one Sunday, I looked up at Jesus hanging on the cross with blood dripping from his limbs, and questioned the sensibility of it all.

"God sent his only begotten son to save us from our sins." I'd heard these words thousands of times without ever thinking about their logic.

Once Paul had said, "If I'd sent my only son to be crucified for any reason, I'd be deemed uncivilized; If any woman today said that God came down from heaven and placed His son in her womb, she'd be considered mentally ill."

Where did all this come from? The Bible had been written, translated again and again into hundreds of languages, and each version is thought to be *"The Word."* Now it all seemed crazy to me. In my new binge of critical thinking, I began to question sin—*I don't lie, cheat, or steal; I treat my neighbor as I treat myself; and I always try to be caring and generous—how am I bad enough to require God's son to die for me?* I was pretty sure God would be pretty goddamned happy with me.

Non-believers were seen as immoral and inherently evil, so I kept my mouth shut about my questions. Ambivalence prevailed.

I continued to do right for *right's sake,* no longer with a promise of heaven or salvation. My spirituality became more grounded in love and I was convinced that this would be enough to save me from the fires of hell.

Though additional questions kept popping up, my faith was ingrained in me, and I couldn't bring myself to betray Jesus—he was part of my "religious DNA." And besides, my in-laws were coming from Massachusetts for Susan's baptism; it didn't feel like the right time to give up religion.

Chapter Twenty-One

Alignment

On Saturdays I went to the A&P to buy groceries —always a pleasure to me. Paul watched Chris and Lisa, and I pushed the baby around in the cart.

One of the highlights was seeing a cashier named Barbara Gladney. Even when her checkout line was long, I'd wait to get in her lane. After a few months of grocery store exchange, I felt like Barbara and I were friends. She was a warm and charming African American woman.

This Saturday morning Barbara asked, "Will you come for tea tomorrow afternoon?"

"Love to," I said. She gave me her phone number and I called her after she finished her shift at four.

I was relieved that we were meeting at Barbara's house rather than in our *dump*. I ventured across the railroad tracks to the other side of town and knocked on Barbara's door. After a minute or two I knocked again and she greeted me. "I'm so sorry it took me so long," she said. "I just got back from church and had to change my shoes—they were killing me. I'm in church from nine to one every Sunday. I think I owe the Lord that, because he treats me really well. But, I don't think he expects me to wear my shoes for the rest of the day."

We sat in two wicker love seats facing each other on a cozy, old fashioned screened-in porch. She offered me a cup of tea from the pot on the table, and a cupcake, and told me she was happy I'd come.

"I've wanted to get to know you better for awhile—I was so happy with your invitation," I said.

The conversation flowed easily. We talked about where we grew up and about her family. Her mother, Mrs. Bradford, was a preacher and ran a food and clothing pantry out of her garage just around the corner. Barbara had a son Tommy and her husband Tom was a police officer in Albion.

When we'd exhausted the preliminaries I said, "Maybe we should plan to go out together some night. It sounds like our husbands will like each other; maybe we could go to a local club, it'd be fun."

When I looked up Barbara's face had turned cold. After a moment of hesitation she said, "Tom and I aren't welcome in any of the clubs in town. None of them accept black people."

"Are you serious?" I asked.

Barbara seemed embarrassed and as she searched for words, she sat up straight on the seat. "We're going to start an all black club so we have a place to go," she explained. "We've been wanting to do this for awhile."

"Is it stupid to think that we could set up a club for people who aren't bigoted?" I asked.

Barbara's face lit up, and we went on to talk about how we could create an alternative. She said she didn't think there were white people who would be interested in such an opportunity, and I assured her that I knew many people who would love the opportunity to know her and her friends.

"Let's work together on this," she offered quietly.

"Yeah, let's! Doing it together will be fabulous—I'd love it."

Barbara and I decided we would meet with Paul and her husband Tom at our house. We set a date for dinner on the following Tuesday night.

As I moved toward my car Barbara yelled out to me. "Tom and I will see you soon, and thanks for coming."

"Thanks for the invite," I replied.

I got in the car, opened the window, and as the car rolled back out of the driveway, I said, "Bring your son Tommy. He and Lisa can play."

Albion was different from where I grew up. I'd known about racism when I lived in Braintree, and to some degree I'd experienced it due to being dark-skinned. When my brother and I were young, we spent a lot of time outside. By the end of the summer we could have passed for black. Some children teased us by calling us "the N word." Nonetheless, I was stunned to realize that bigotry was so present in this town.

Where we grew up in Braintree it was like the TV show, "Happy Days," homogeneous, with few black families.

A black boy sat next to me in English class. I don't recall his name, but he seemed lonely and distant. I was nice to him, but his discomfort was visceral, and my efforts to help him feel more comfortable seemed to make things worse. Nobody bothered him, but they didn't reach out either. It was like he didn't exist.

One of my Scottish relatives told me not to wear red, because it made me look darker, and less pretty. The lesson I *internalized* was that being light-skinned meant being good *and* pretty—and that I wasn't light enough or good enough—or pretty. As I got older, my skin lightened, but the lesson had been "learned."

It wasn't easy to sort through it all. But when I talked to Barbara, I began to think critically for the first time about racism, and I came to realize that it had been *cultivated* in me. I determined that I would never allow it to show its ugly face. No options; to deny its existence would have negated ever making it go away.[8]

It disturbed me, but it was naïve to think that more than twenty years of indoctrination would be wiped out in an instant. So I decided that my every action would be put through a filter of equality, with the hope that it could change me, and change the world.

Barbara and Tom arrived promptly at six on Tuesday with their son and a homemade sweet potato pie. I'd fed the kids and put Chris and Susan to bed just before they arrived. Their little boy Tommy was adorable with a round face and bright eyes.

"Come on," Lisa said. "Let's play—come with me."

Our daughter was confident and gregarious with big blue eyes and loosely-curled, light brown hair. She grabbed Tommy's hand and pulled him into the small crappy den nearby.

Barbara's husband Tom was a quiet, pleasant-looking guy who seemed comfortable with us.

Paul had wanted me to make pasta with clam sauce; Paul *always* wanted pasta with clam sauce. But the smell of the rib roast and roasted vegetables permeating the house, and the promise of the sweet potato pie was lovely enough to ease his disappointment.

As we ate, we planned, and by the time we got to Barbara's pie we decided to call our new club the *Melting Pot*. We also agreed that the name would require a consensus, and that the club would be purely social, free of political agendas—and above all—fun.

"Do you want us to have the first dinner here?" I asked.

Paul chimed in. "I think it would be better for us to start; we should be the ones to put ourselves out there first."

---

8   For more information on racial bias, see: *Psychology Today:* "Between the lines; Perspectives of race, culture, and community." By Lihail Lyubansky, PH.D.

"Yeah", Tom replied. "I think some of our friends might be a little skeptical in the beginning, but they'll come along, and it gives a good message."

Barbara then interjected. "Let's make it a pot-luck and ask everyone to bring their best dishes. It'll be cheaper, and you won't have to cook. If it works, others will be more willing to have events at *their* houses in the future."

When the Gladneys left we were all excited at the possibility of making things better.

A little concern crept back into my consciousness about having a big dinner party in our *bummer* house, but I again reminded myself that it would be shallow and dumb to let it interfere with such an important opportunity. We had, after all, finished the rooms that would be most used for the party.

Paul and I had worked together to take the layers of disgusting navy blue paint off the kitchen cabinets, woodwork, and large bay window casing above the sink. It had been a *bitch* to scrape the layers and layers of painted wallpaper off the dining room ceiling —it was white now thanks to Paul's hard work. His shoulder froze up for awhile after the job was done. Then he placed faux brick behind the stove area. It all looked great to me.

I didn't care about the small and dirty old den and the closet-like half bath now that things were in perspective—*a toilet is a toilet,* I told myself, *as long as it flushes.*

Barbara and Tom invited three couples and Paul and I did the same, totaling sixteen at the first Melting Pot dinner. First to arrive was Tom carrying a huge platter of southern fried chicken, Barbara right behind him.

Then came Dick Powell, an Assistant Principal of Albion High School, and his wife Sylvia. After Dr. Martin Luther King had been shot, Dick had to deal with the challenges and turmoil in the high school, and it was difficult for him. As a black man he identified with how the students felt—disadvantaged and marginalized— but it was his job to hold them accountable—and he did.

Sylvia, a teacher, was a reserved woman of few words, but we knew she was totally invested in our new club by the way she listened and nodded her head when we talked about our ideas.

Several of our friends came in after the Powells and the Gladneys. I could always depend on my good friend Pat Stumpff to make people feel comfortable. She was a stay-at-home-mom like me, and our kids often played together. Her husband was a good friend as well. He was a brilliant engineer at the plant and Paul and I liked him very much.

We made some new friends that first night. High School shop teacher Arthell Wyette, a friend of Tom and Barbara's was a small man, but I sensed a big presence. He talked about the conflict he felt. It was similar to Dick Powell's, and I understood it. Arthell was married to Gloria, the most guarded person in the room; I found her to be cordial, but inscrutable.

Almost all the couples had arrived on time. Tommy Thornton (Tommy T) and his wife Dorothy were the last of Barbara and Tom's friends to show up for dinner. Tommy worked with Paul and Dorothy was a teacher, and they were a handsome couple.

As Tommy T walked in, Dick chided him. "You're always late for everything, you're giving people the idea that what they say about black people is true—are you *ever* on time?"

Dorothy laughed—she turned out to be easy to like.

The combination of guests worked; they were comfortable with one another. The night became almost jovial. We mingled and had a great time talking about life and kids and the world. Drinking cheap wine, we played "Ain't It Awful," commiserating about the challenges of parenthood.

Barbara threw the Melting Pot name out, and the group accepted it. The stipulation was that its purpose was to have "fun," without any political agenda.

The meal was fabulous—Barbara's southern fried chicken and sweet potato pie were a huge hit, and her friends brought collard greens and other tasty dishes including a big dish of *chitlins* that all the black people in the room seemed to relish. I made spaghetti with clam sauce, (so Paul was happy). My friends made biscuits, salads, vegetable dishes, and casseroles. We set the conglomeration of food on a buffet table and everyone got to try everything.

When the evening was over, I felt great. Even the dining room had felt kind of nice; when the lights were dimmed and the candles were lit, it looked warm and welcoming.

Arthell and Gloria agreed to have the next party at their house in two months. Each couple was to invite one new couple.

Gloria and Arthell lived on the outskirts of town, and when we arrived Gloria was still scrubbing the bathroom—I could relate.

Directly behind the house was a good-sized piece of land. Arthell had built a campfire, and put chairs around it. Tommy T was late again, and the group all teased him about it. Several new couples joined us at this party, and the dinner was once again a multi-ethnic gourmet delight.

"Paul and Sandy, try Dorothy's chitlins," Tommy T insisted.

"No offense, Tom, but chitlins remind me of my Italian grandmother's tripe—it was the only thing she ever cooked that I didn't like," I answered.

"Yeah, but you haven't tried *Dorothy's* chitlins. Paul, you absolutely have to try the chitlins," Tommy insisted.

"OK, OK, give me a few damn *chitlins*, but if I don't like them I don't want Dorothy to feel bad. Sometimes people just don't like things."

"I promise I won't, Paul," Dorothy said, "and don't try them on *my* account."

Sylvia Powell told Tommy T he needed to leave us alone as Paul put a few on his plate and tasted them; he didn't like them.

Sylvia again chided Tommy T. "Now why did you go and make the poor man try something he didn't like? Sometimes I wonder about you."

I then took a couple of them from Paul's plate, tasted them, and joked—"It's a good thing I wasn't a slave. I think I'da starved." Everyone laughed.

People seemed to be having fun in the banter, and in the end, the party was a success.

I liked everyone at Arthell and Gloria's house, except for two white women who gave me a bad vibe. Their body language was closed and they only talked to one another. One of them had been in the JC-ettes. One husband worked at the plant, and the other owned a small business in town. The men seemed more comfortable than their wives.

In the following week I saw one of the women at the market, and in the course of conversation she said, "You *talk* like them when you're with them."

I strategically responded. "I don't know what you mean by *like them?*"

She was oblivious and answered. "I mean like *them*, the *blacks*."

"I guess I do speak differently when I'm partying. There's a certain fun in the banter that makes me feel happy. And besides, I don't think of friends as *them*—Is the way I interact with my friends a problem for you?" I asked gently.

"Problem? No, not really," she responded with some discomfort. As the Melting Pot grew, both women from the party realized that they were in the minority. It's possible that because their husbands were invested in the group, they kept attending.

It wasn't long before the Melting Pot got too big for anyone's home. Soon the other segregated clubs started losing members. Word was out that they were exclusionary and that we had better food, better music, and more fun at our parties. Many people wanted to disassociate themselves with the racist clubs.

The Mayor, the Chief of Police, teachers and administrators from the high school, the manager of the plant, and executives and union members from various businesses all joined The Melting Pot.

In addition, we had members from two fine institutions: *Starr Commonwealth*, a treatment program for troubled kids, and *Albion College*. It was an amazing mix of local people.

In time our group grew so big that we had to rent a large hall to accommodate the crowd. We appointed officers and established club dues. The food continued to be donated, and it was always incredible; it was like our first dinner, just more of it.

In the fall, scheduling a Melting Pot Halloween party required extensive organization because we had to make arrangements for music, decorations, and food for two hundred people. Everyone came in costume, and the decorations included the usual skeletons and pumpkins. Dressed as Elvis, Paul walked by a table and heard two men arguing. He thought there was a problem.

He soon learned that the two were debating about whether the Detroit Lions would win the up and coming game; one was the Mayor and one of only a few Jewish people in town, and the other was a black union representative.

One of the first community events scheduled after the formation of the Melting Pot, was a beauty pageant to choose "Miss Albion." The city manager asked me to organize and run it, so I asked several Melting Pot members to be judges, and had them design the criteria to determine the winner. We all agreed that there would be no bathing suit competition.

In those days beauty pageants were big, and white girls always won. The event was held in the high school auditorium and on the night of the pageant the room was packed full of students and community members. People were turned away at the door, and most of the audience was young.

The tension in the room was palpable. People feared violence, and the black kids, in particular, were sure that the process of choosing "Miss Albion" wouldn't be fair.

I had asked Daniel Bogan, a brilliant, young black intellectual in his late twenties, to be a judge. I felt if he helped to plan and execute the event, there would be an assurance that the results would be fair.

When Dan joined the Melting Pot, he had a reputation as an activist with few apologies. He was angry about the oppression of

African Americans. Some believed Dan was too angry, but Paul and I were not among them.

Dan's wife Libby was more militant than he was, and would have no part of the Melting Pot. After several pleas, I gave up. But Libby and I remained friends.

At the Halloween party she had shown up unannounced. "You didn't invite me to this party—why didn't you invite me?" she asked.

I responded to her whining with confidence; I was tired of her antics. "Sometimes Libby, you can be a colossal pain in the ass. If I had invited you to the party, you wouldn't have come. You said the Melting Pot was worthless and that you would never come to a party or dinner. Obviously you didn't need an invitation to come here tonight, because you're here. People just *come* because they want to be here. I'm glad you're here, in fact I'm ecstatic, but come on—sometimes I think you like making me feel bad."

She knew I was right, as she sat there with an impish smile on her face. She didn't respond. It was at this Halloween event that I began to confront her actions, and we were both better for it.

Dan sat with the other judges as the room filled to capacity. There were ten judges—five were black and five white.

I came out onto the stage smiling, held two thumbs up, and boldly introduced myself. "Hello everyone, I'm Sandy and I'm the MC tonight—we're going to have a great time together and witness these beautiful girls perform some fabulous talent." There was applause and then quiet—I was happy.

I opened the event with a hippy-dippy song,

> What the world needs now Is love sweet love.
> That's the only thing that there's just too little of . . . [9]

I could feel the ice break a bit as I sang, in spite of the fact that the song was totally hokey.

---

9   http://www.metrolyrics.com/what-the-world-needs-now-is-love-lyrics-jackie-deshannon.html

Our contestants were all pretty—six black girls and seven white; each was required to perform in the talent showcase. When I introduced them, there was a noticeable buzz in the room and it was building—I was irritated.

As I introduced the girls one at a time, they lined up on the stage. While there wasn't out-right heckling, anxiety and even fear was palpable with each irreverent loud comment.

The girls left the stage and I introduced the first performance—a modern dancer. She danced across the stage in spite of the noisy audience. At first I thought it was because she was white, but then the noise didn't stop when the second girl came out. I wondered if the black kids were being rude to white girls, or vice versa, because the audience was still making a racket during the second performance.

"Please quiet down," I pleaded. They didn't. Before I introduced the third young woman, I stood with the microphone for several minutes. I waited and waited some more—the audience kept buzzing on loudly. I was incensed.

Becoming the proverbial mother for an audience of 500 kids, I said, "I'm not going on with this until you're quiet. These girls deserve better. It takes a lot of courage to be up here on stage—respect is basic, it's important. Please be nice."

Within seconds, there was silence. I was relieved.

"OK now, let's go on and enjoy the show."

After that, everything was fine. At one point one of the contestants asked me if I'd announce that she had lost a valuable ring that belonged to her mother. I did, and it was found. The contestant, a pretty black girl, was ecstatic—I held up the ring and the crowd roared.

All the girls performed, and then, while the scores were being tallied, I sang another song—almost as hokey as the first.

> Think of your fellow man.
> Give him a helping hand.

Put a little love In your heart. [10]

In retrospect, it's surprising they didn't throw tomatoes.

It was then time to announce the finalists. When I opened the envelope I learned that two were black and three were white. As I announced their names, the audience applauded loudly for each.

The tenor in the room had completely changed; a totally sexist process was effective in addressing a totally racist process—what irony.

Then came the "Q & A" segment of the pageant. The questions had been designed by the judges to reflect the characters of the finalists.

The first contestant was a young white woman named Paula. I opened the card with the first question. "Miss Paula, do you have an obligation to use your talents to help others?"

The young woman thought for a moment and then answered: "The world is complicated right now, and sometimes we have trouble understanding each other—I'm not sure my talent is big enough to change things significantly, but whatever I can do, I'll do. If we all do the same, the world will be better. *Yes,* I feel it's my duty to do what I can with the few talents I have." The audience applauded appropriately.

The questions went on, and each was as compelling as the one before. Most of the girls answered their questions thoughtfully and with grace. But, some answered with greater sophistication.

After more deliberation from the judges, I stood with the results in hand. The five candidates had been whittled down to four. The room was silent. "The third runner up is"—a black teen named Geana, with a gorgeous shape and sparkling eyes came to the center. She didn't seem surprised—she hadn't done well enough on her question to win—and she knew it.

I went on. The second runner-up Miss Jody, was a blue-eyed, blond girl. As she stepped forward and stood next to Miss

10 http://www.metrolyrics.com/put-a-little-love-in-your-heart-lyrics-jackie-deshannon.html

Geana—she looked crushed. Perhaps she expected to win. Blue-eyed blonds were often selected as "most beautiful."

This left two contestants, one black and the other white. Both had impressed everyone when they answered the questions, but Miss Paula had been particularly articulate. She was relatively attractive but not gorgeous, and her figure was average, but understated in a charming way. It was clear that she had the perfect answer to her question. The other runner-up, Miss Latitia, was a full-bodied, confident, and lovely young African-American woman with a beautiful face. She had answered her question well, but not as well as Miss Paula.

When I announced the winner, the audience cheered. Miss Paula stood in shock as she took the crown and flowers; Miss Paula had become *Miss Albion*—it was done.

When the audience filed out, they smiled and talked to each other amicably.

As I approached Dan, he quietly said, "It was a totally fair event—*totally fair*." Barbara agreed. She had also been a judge.

I could see Dan's wife Libby behind him sulking, and when she came over during the following week with her kids, we talked about the pageant. She had an interesting viewpoint. She said the judges were prejudiced—"Black girls have big butts, and the judges held it against the first runner up," she proclaimed.

After thinking about the beauty pageant I wondered if the end justified the means—it couldn't be good to find primary identity in beauty, or to glorify vanity. I knew first hand because my family had always focused on such things. To my mother, in particular, pretty was everything. From the time I was a small child, when she was combing my tangled curly hair, she'd say, "You have to suffer to be beautiful." The family didn't really care about intellect, as long as I got by in school. But they'd believed I had good looks, and in their eyes, as a woman, that's all I'd need. I recalled the agony of my adolescence and my own pageant experience.

I started thinking about "The Miss Albion" contest. *Maybe it had been a bad idea for these girls*, I thought, with a twinge of guilt. The pageant catalyzed my awareness of what it meant to be a woman—the seed of feminism was growing.

We had a workshop after the pageant to talk about what young women see in their futures, and a "sleep in" was held at the Armory with girls who were high school juniors.

The participants talked about life, and their futures and they listened to music—they got to know each other. Police officers hung around outside to be sure no boys came around with ideas.

A few teachers who were members of the Melting Pot helped to monitor the event. The group learned to take turns playing music of different genres. For the first time Latin faces and culture came into the picture; it was a truly multi-cultural event.

At one point the dean of Albion College called Paul and me to ask if we could take a young, racially mixed couple into our home. "She's from Jamaica and graduated, but her husband won't graduate until May," he explained. "They don't have much money; they need a place until the end of the semester. Can you help them?"

John and Georgiana Patterson arrived that night with suitcases in hand. She was tall with a cropped Afro, beautiful West Indian skin, and bright eyes. He was pale, skinny, and timid, and a scraggly beard lined his cheeks. Georgiana was a powerhouse. They were an unlikely pair.

We struck a deal. In exchange for rent Georgiana would help with the baby and the housework while John finished college.

Georgiana began doing housework immediately, and took every opportunity to take care of Susan. In the mornings she would steal her out of bed, and when I came down with the other kids for breakfast, she would have the baby fed and spotless. She soon fell in love with the baby, and in essence became Susan's nanny.

I'd been brought up to believe that women took care of their own infants until they were in school. But the fact that Georgiana was competent and caring made me think differently; it didn't take long to happily allow an ideal nanny with a college degree to care for my baby while I continued to work in the community.

Paul's parents Fred and Dorothy came to visit while Georgiana and John lived with us. It was Georgiana's idea to put a white apron on and jokingly act like the maid. Fred didn't like it, and when he realized that an interracial couple lived with us, he decided to fly back to Boston as soon as possible.

The night before his departure, Fred and Paul fought about race and culture in America, and that sealed the deal. For the first time Paul had stepped from under his father's influence and control.

It was particularly aggravating for Fred to leave before Susan's baptism because we had postponed it so that he and my mother in-law could be there. I didn't understand them wanting to come because they were Catholic, and Susan was to be christened in the Episcopal Church. Then I remembered that my mother-in-law's own mother had been the daughter of a Protestant.

I would have bagged the whole christening in view of my newly established religious awakening, but my mother-in-law, bless her heart, chose to stay on her own. I had no idea she had the courage to stand up to "King Fred," and I admired her for it. After the baptism Paul's mother went home.

For me, I had finally come to grips with my religious *DNA*. The baptism was our last formal involvement with church. We attended weddings and funerals of those we loved, but that was the extent of church-related activities.

During John and Georgiana's stay with us, I hadn't seen John much. Because of the confusion at our house, he always studied at the library. But Georgiana was always around, and it was fun for me to have a friend to talk to while Paul was working long hours.

John was no match for Georgiana; when I saw them argue on several occasions, she always won.

On a rainy night in the last week of their stay, I heard Georgiana yelling, and when I went down to the den where they were staying, I saw that she'd clawed John's face with her fingernails.

Just as I entered the room, Georgiana leaped for his throat. I pulled her off him, and told her that this *could not* happen in my house, and *should not* happen anywhere. She was breathing heavily and there was still fire in her eyes, but when she looked at me, she calmed down. I had to acknowledge to myself that Georgiana was a batterer. I didn't know anything about handling domestic violence. Few people did. I was happy that she and her husband were leaving—it was time.

John graduated from college in late May, as planned, and he and Georgiana left following the graduation ceremony.

In just three and a half years, diverse groups of people in Albion had come to know each other; new friendships and networks had developed that would have been presumed impossible—progress was undeniable.

Independent programs began popping up all over the place. Johnson Day Care Center was built with donations, an entirely volunteer ambulance service was established to serve the area, and volunteers founded a citizen-operated museum. New networks brought new innovation and equal opportunity began to be seen in the community's governing bodies including on the city council and school board.

Albion had become an exciting place to live. An annual celebration, the *Festival of the River Forks*, was established—a final testimony of success.

When Paul learned he'd been promoted to a new position in Big Flats, New York, I'd been vomiting for a week. "I think I'm pregnant," I said.

"You always think you're pregnant."

"I always *am* pregnant."

When I returned home from the doctor with the confirmation, Paul started—"Well we chose to go on the vacation with the money we saved instead of using it for a vasectomy—it was that damned vacation."

Susan's delivery was fresh in my mind, and while the idea of having another baby was OK, the idea of going through another delivery—oh, my God!

While many women have choices—well let's just say I was destined to have another child.

I was sad to leave Albion; the transformation of the little city led us to believe that we could be agents of change—with friends and neighbors we had transformed a community of de-facto segregation that would ultimately become a national model. While we helped to change Albion, Albion had changed us, and we would never again be the same.

PART 3

CHAPTER TWENTY-TWO

Blind Acceptance and Stark Reality

The quiet and totally white nature of our new home was anti-climactic after the excitement of the previous several years. Big Flats, New York was a suburban neighborhood that housed a bunch of nice white people who liked eating gourmet food and playing golf on the weekends. We found little culture and no color, and we were challenged to find meaning in the emptiness of prosperity.

We had lived in our new home for seven months when our youngest daughter Joanie was born. *"Don't let it happen again,"* I yelled, as they wheeled me into the delivery room. I had explained the horror of my last experience to my new doctor during an appointment with him; I couldn't have taken a repeat childbirth episode.

The delivery room team quickly put a mask on my face, and bang—I magically had a baby girl in my arms when I woke up.

As we'd named Susan after Paul's older sister, we decided to continue the tradition. We named the new baby after his sister Joan, and we agreed on the perfect middle name for a pretty combination—Joan Dorothy Pimentel.

I could think of no better names to give two daughters.

My nights were spent feeding Joanie, and changing her and Susan's diapers, and because there was bed-wetting, I had sheets to change as well. To add insult to injury, Lisa was a sleep-walker, and I was constantly keeping an eye open for fear that she would get into trouble while sleeping. I didn't get much sleep back then.

Paul's sister Joanie had come from California to be with the kids while I was in the hospital. She had engaged the kids in making *Welcome Home Mommy and Baby* signs and homemade *happy* cards. None of the children showed any sign of jealousy when Joanie was born; I did my best to make them all feel like this was their baby, too. There were only thirteen months between Susan and Joanie. They were both good babies, and that helped.

During the year and a half we spent in New York, I was primarily a wife and mother, except for the one night a week when I volunteered on a suicide hot line. I worked Tuesdays and Paul worked Thursdays, when he wasn't at the office.

During our stint there, we ate some very good food as members of a gourmet club, but beyond that, there was little of interest to do. The people were nice, but we missed the sense of community and diversity that we'd found in Albion.

One night while working at the crisis center, a man called in threatening to shoot himself in the head. "I hate life, I hate myself, and I don't want to live another minute."

I talked to him, and after a few minutes of effort, the man miraculously agreed to wait until someone could come to his house to help talk him through to the other side of his anguish before he made an irreversible decision.

When I arrived at his house, two mental health crisis workers pulled into the driveway at the same time. By the time the police arrived, they had helped the man to calm down and accept help. He had put the gun into the caseworker's hands and fallen to the floor in mournful hysteria. I hadn't seen a gun since the Watts riots, and felt the presence of it, as the caseworker held it safely in his palm.

I wasn't sufficiently trained to do work of this magnitude, and shouldn't have been asked to deal with such a situation. I had much more confidence than I had any right to have—this attitude would serve as a theme for my life. Fortunately, in this instance, my instincts were enough; I was lucky.

I longed for my family and friends in New England, and missed the friends and vitality of community life we had left behind. Our high school friends, the Goldbergs, Dands, and Langs came to visit and it provided a visceral connection to home. It served as a band-aid to my longing. My most exciting pastime was to sit on our lovely screened back porch as my children watched the squirrels collecting nuts for the winter.

We did, however, have a number of visits from Fred and Dorothy. The negative experiences with Fred in Albion had left a bad taste. It was difficult to welcome him with open arms, but I did it anyway. Dorothy, on the other hand, was always a delight.

After Joanie's birth, Paul and I decided to use more discretion, so he scheduled a vasectomy with a local surgeon. When his parents came to visit, Paul told his father what he was planning, and Fred was horrified at such drastic action: "I would never do such a thing!"

We couldn't understand Fred's reaction. The next day I was chatting with him and realized that he didn't know what a vasectomy was, and thought Paul intended to be castrated.

That night we were lying in bed laughing as Paul said, "I can't believe my father thought that I was going to have my balls cut off!"

During our stay in Albion we had visited home at least once a year, and our parents came to visit us occasionally. As time went on I came to see the dichotomy in our families, and thus, to better understand *myself*.

From the very beginning Paul's father had much more influence over my life than he should have; Paul never admitted how his father made *him* feel, and in the beginning he wasn't able to see how his dad affected me, either.

Fred was—in many ways—a complex man. When he'd arrived at age twelve in America from the Portuguese Island of Fayal in 1919, he went into a kind of social rebellion. He stopped speaking his native language and denied any identification with his heritage and culture. His entire family had learned to speak English without an accent from a French tutor in the Azores, so he was already ahead of other immigrants in that regard.

As a young teenager Fred would cross the street in Fall River, Massachusetts to avoid being recognized by other Portuguese "peasants" who might be walking toward him. By his standards, he was different; he had come from an educated family and therefore, he considered himself above others.

When I'd met Fred, the only evidence of his heritage I noted was his love of linguica[11] and beans, and he ate them every Saturday afternoon without fail.

Most of the time I loved the Italian side of me, but when I was with Fred I became *like* him. In those moments I *too* hid from my identity in order to be someone else. Paul's father made it clear by his patronizing attitude toward my father, that he thought Italians were inferior; I felt subjugated rather than angered by that attitude. Fred further reinforced my feelings of inferiority. So my self-appointed mission became to convince him (and me) that I was *not inferior*.

Fred often talked down to me and wouldn't admit that I was a thinker. In essence, he didn't believe that women had value beyond the duties of a wife and mother.

For many years I remained trapped. I wanted to belong. But I knew that my being accepted was contingent on doing everything that Fred wanted me to do when I was in his presence. So that's what I tried to do.

---

11 Traditional Portuguese pork sausage made with a large amount of paprika

I think it was their family rituals that eventually propelled me towards truth. By that time we had children and lived far away. But when we visited, or he visited, he controlled.

The need to line us up on the top of the stairs on Christmas morning, like we were five, the exercise of doing everything in exactly the same way every day, and the placing of every house-hold item in its exact spot, without an inch of deviation, was stifling. In the end I realized that life without creativity and spontaneity has little meaning, and that such a fettered structure can deplete one's soul.

The bottom line was that Fred made me feel inadequate. He made me think that I was unable to boil an egg or make a cup of tea without supervision. If I had been more secure, I would have let him take control and been done with it. But I wasn't secure.

In many ways the little everyday rituals and requirements were designed to insulate Fred, his wife Dorothy, and their children from the rest of the world. While people loved to be at my parents' house, they felt uncomfortable at Fred's, because somehow they knew he didn't want them there. As a result, their family remained isolated. Paul and *our children* were welcome, but *I* was more of a requirement than a happy addition.

It would be years before my personal growth would allow me to psychologically separate from Fred's dominance.

Paul was truly a good man, and those who knew him realized he was a teddy bear. But when he was in his twenties, he could bulldoze his ideas over others—not unlike Fred. During our stay in New York, Paul's company sent him to a sort of "charm school for smart guys who thought they knew everything." In the workshop he had assumed that the quiet guy in the corner didn't know as much as he did. During the group process, Paul had been trying to push his answers on everyone for hours. Suddenly he realized the quiet guy had the correct solution to the problem they were pondering. Sometimes you think you know everything and you know nothing.

The lessons at the school were very helpful in grooming him to be an effective manager, and to help him realize he wasn't the only one in the world with an original thought that might have merit. It was to Paul's advantage and a gift to our relationship that he learned to stop perpetuating one of Fred's least admirable traits.

By the time Paul switched jobs and went with another firm, we had moved out of New York. By then, we had known each other for seventeen years, and had been married for seven of them.

In the first three years of marriage when Paul was in the Navy, we only spent three months together, but we managed to have two children, and after his discharge, we quickly had two more.

By our sixth year of marriage we were twenty-nine years old, had four children, had lived in five apartments, and owned two houses.

Paul and I were accustomed to looking for places to live, and while housing was as scarce in our newly assigned town of Wynton as it had been in Albion, we were determined not to spend months in suspended animation.

While driving around looking for an independent listing, we came across a house in the middle of town with a small *for sale* sign on it. I'm not sure where the kids were on that day when I walked up the few stairs to the door of the house and knocked gently.

A pretty woman named Mary answered the door. She was in her mid thirties, and had short light hair and green eyes. When I asked her how we could make arrangements to see the house, she invited me in for a spontaneous tour. I signaled for Paul to join me.

A small entrance area at the top of the stairs led into the living room. It was cluttered, and we used our imaginations to picture the room without the mess. The walls were an easy shade of celery green and plush carpeting and indirect lighting created a warm and comfortable ambiance. We both determined that it was lovely underneath it all.

We waded through junk as we passed through a nice dining room. When we reached the kitchen, dirty pots and pans and old food—fried eggs and pancake batter—covered the stove and counters around it.

On the floor sat an enormous pile of dog poo. The dog had to be the size of a horse. Mary just walked around the poop and said

"Sorry," in a way that was barely apologetic. When I glanced at the pile again, I thought, *this woman has a hell of a stomach!*

Viewing the rest of the house we came upon a beautiful Saint Bernard with a pixy face and charming disposition.

"She's a girl, but we call her Charlie."

I said, "Hi" to Charlie, and patted her gently.

Mary showed us the "office" side of the house. She said her husband was a physician and he planned to move his office when the house was sold.

There was less clutter, but this part of the house truly needed cosmetic surgery; the three rooms were dark and dated, their walls a dull and dirty gray. In the first room was a black leather examining table.

Mary then took us upstairs. In a number of the six large bedrooms, the doctor's papers completely carpeted the hardwood floors with only a glimpse of wood peaking through here and there.

When we returned for a second visit, Mary's husband, Dr. Ivan, was there as well. The fireplace was lit, classical music was playing, and the house was somewhat cleaner.

The handsome, young doctor took us up to the attic, which was the size of a skating rink. The very large building had once been a duplex; there were double staircases and secret passages throughout.

After little consideration, we bought the house. Structurally, it was sound and the price was low. The living room, dining room, and kitchen had been completely refinished, and were very nice. Even though we had little need for fourteen rooms, we considered it a good investment.

Our house was located around the corner from stores, restaurants, and a bar. City Hall, which contained the jail, was diagonally across the street. We often heard drunken hunters carrying on after a day of drinking and trying to kill deer. Those fortunate enough to have had a kill enjoyed the envy of the rest as they socialized in the square.

Guns were a cultural tag for some of the locals; they were everywhere, seen as a necessity, and available to almost anyone. Many men (and some women) hung rifles in their trucks—handy for hunting and for protection from a variety of real and perceived dangers. Rattlesnakes inhabited the hills and thousands were either shot or captured each year and thrown into a huge pit to be milked for venom.

Living in a factory town had its advantages. Paul met new people immediately at work, and I soon met their wives. All of Paul's colleagues belonged to the Wynton Country Club and there was a lot of pressure for us to join.

Because there was virtually nothing else in town to do, and everyone *we* knew socialized there, we had joined the club—reluctantly. It was also the only place where our kids could swim and play with other friends they knew. I had bought golf clubs so that Paul and I could play golf together; we lost every single ball we hit on our first day on the course, and used the "F" word on every green. By this time it was OK for both of us to express ourselves freely. Paul had announced that he would never play golf with me again.

In Wynton partying or working were among the few options. So, the first thing we did was throw a party. We invited fifteen people over on a Friday night for a painting party, and asked them to bring whatever paint they had hanging around the house—bright colors totally acceptable.

The plant manager, Charles, showed up with a bucket, his best paintbrush, and some white paint he expected to use with precision.

But precision wasn't what we had in mind. We didn't care about the fourteenth room in our house—we had to walk through two other rooms to get there; we knew we would never use it, and that it would be easy to throw a coat of paint on it before we moved away to yet another remote place in the universe.

Paul and I were ready for a *real* party and instructed everyone to paint whatever they wanted on the walls. People drank too much. Some were meticulous, while others just threw the paint on the walls like abstract artists.

When people left they were very happy, and the walls were covered with flowers, trees, and people—one of them, a nude woman.

It had been a fun creative adventure, and when it was over, I closed the door knowing that we would never use the room again. I did however, paint over the naked lady the next day, to make her look like little Miss Sunshine on her way to church. The room became an art gallery seldom seen, but occasionally I'd walk through it and smile.

There was so much space for the kids to play in our new house; they always had choices. If I was working in the kitchen, I'd let them run around on the office side, because it was easy for me to keep an eye on them. We converted one of the large bedrooms on the second floor into a great den for toys and a television, and they would ride their bicycles around in the attic every day.

While the house felt vast and sometimes creepy, Paul and I had a beautiful rose-colored bedroom with a huge bay window, and it became my cozy sanctuary.

After the first six months in our new home, I fell into a funk. As my world of mops, diapers, and the stove became drudgery, my depression became more palpable. We'd made some friends quickly, but the town felt unwelcoming and different from any place we'd ever known. Paul worked constantly and was seldom home, so I felt alone and isolated.

To help me get through my depression, I wrote poems about feeling really miserable and wanting a different life. Some were self indulgent and pathetic, but they often inspired me to stay balanced and to recognize that my situation was a rite of passage.

MOTHERHOOD
My home is my heaven and my hell.
I love my husband completely and respectfully with passion;
my children with joyful delight and tenderness.
It's hard not to live— today—everything you are and will be.
I work. I do, but seem to do nothing.
I help my children to love everyone, but often ask myself if it's enough.
In spite of this I'm still me, a stem whose buds cannot and should not
fully come forth
for fear of hurting the fragile plant beneath.
It's my responsibility now, to be what I must be—a woman like most,
but not as the few.
I'm only one person, damn it, damn it—I want to be two.
Oh, to be two. To be what I am—and what I am.
To do what I want—and what I want.
While my life lacks expression,
I know that my loving will lend to goodness in society and for humanity.
This is me now, but not tomorrow;
time will lead to a different mode of living for me.
I'm a mother
whose day will come.

A picture paints a 1000 words

The next chapter in our lives is difficult to contemplate. A life-long question has been asked time and time again by all those who love us and who know the story of Frank and Julius, the two young men who lived with us in 1972—"Why did you make such reckless choices?"

While I've never adequately been able to answer this question, I can only say that it always seemed easy to dance on the edge of reason when it came to blindly accepting people.

I prided myself with being a good mother—nurturing and protective, but later I had to think long and hard about the question posed to me by my friends, and own that my confidence was arrogant in the face of the risks to my family and to myself.

When Paul and I left Albion we were feeling empowered, positive, and filled with hope. Our optimism only served as a liability for what occurred after we left Albion and then New York.

In our new home in Wynton, life reeled out of control like a malignancy when we encountered the narrow-minded and unpredictable personalities—the shadow side of human behaviors coalescing.

I, Sandy, hadn't been feeling fine, but, as a wife and mother, I was doing my job and it felt like I was holding up. But, the weight of homesickness in combination with my need to take care of everyone else was taking its toll and while I never shared my feelings with anyone, I felt like I was carrying an anvil around my neck. In fact, I had been depressed for so long, that it really was unrecognizable to me. Most people didn't have any idea what I was feeling, not even Paul. In 1972, I continued to carry the burden of my childhood—intellectual inferiority and sadness. Perhaps these inadequate feelings compelled me to make up the difference by going over the top to help others—I just can't say.

In spite of my insecurities, I always trusted my instincts when it came to how people would treat me, and of how I should treat them. Paul also understood this as being my greatest strength, and always trusted my instincts in this regard.

I think my father had been similarly wired as he frequently picked people up who others might have feared and occasionally brought them home. Like him, I almost always got what I expected from people, and on those few occasions when I didn't, I could talk my way to a viable outcome. In a sense, I embraced the theory of *self-fulfilling prophesy* and it had always worked for me.

By the time Paul and I moved to Wynton, we knew we could *not* change the world; but we'd learned we *could* make a difference.

We heard about a young man named Frank. The fact that he was a recovering drug addict didn't faze us. In our arrogance, we thought we could do our little bit for the world by giving him a place to stay. We never entertained the idea that he would rob us or take drugs while under our roof. And in the end, we were right in this regard. The problem was, survival had been his life-long modus operandi, but what had been strength on the streets of Detroit, was a liability in this little town.

The problem with Frank was relative to the world beyond our walls, and to his perception of survival there. Being African American, having had a drug problem, coming from the streets of Detroit, and living in a small town with some racist people waiting for any excuse to strike, set his fate.

While Paul and I wanted to give Frank every chance, we had little understanding that the threat in this town was unlike any place we had ever lived. We knew it wasn't perfect, but perceived it to be far more gentle than it actually was. This would prove to be Frank's—and later, his brother Julius's—greatest misfortune.

The next chapter in our lives—and in the lives of the two young men who lived with us—continues to be difficult to contemplate.

As Paul and I sat in the living room of our large townhouse in the middle of *nowhere*, Frank, a handsome young African American man in his late teens held his guitar close to his chest and began to sing a "Thank God" version of "The House of the Rising Sun." Frank's voice, though untrained, was remarkably strong and polished, and he'd changed the lyrics to make it more acceptable to the Christian contingency of friends he'd made during his recovery from drug addiction.

He'd gotten "straight" in previous months after completing a *Teen Challenge* drug rehabilitation program. We'd met him through a neighbor—a benevolent, born-again Christian dentist who was invested in helping kids with drug issues.

When Frank completed the rehabilitation program, he needed a place to live. So, the dentist who lived down the street had invited him to live with his family for several weeks.

Frank announced that he was ready to move out of his current home, and asked if we had any ideas. "Now is a good time for me to move on and be more independent," Frank explained.

Paul and I instantly liked Frank—he was a charmer; we agreed that he could move into the attic with the idea that he'd find a job and become independent. Within a few days he was settled.

It didn't take long for Frank to assimilate and feel comfortable with us. The house was huge and the attic private and empty. Frank wasn't the kind of guy who played with the kids, but he was patient and responsive when the opportunity called for him to give them his attention.

After we discussed a plan of action, Frank agreed to follow Paul's advice; he said he would start looking for a job, and we were content with his commitment after he sent out a couple of responses to newspaper ads.

CHAPTER TWENTY-THREE

Nightmare

Frank had been living with us for about two months when he announced he was going to Detroit to visit his family. In spite of trying he hadn't landed a job yet. He drove to Detroit in an old car he'd bought with money he'd borrowed from his sponsor, and within a week, he returned with a surprise.

I was alone in the kitchen when Frank walked in.

"This is my brother, Julius," Frank said. "He wants to get straight; he wants to be like me." While Frank and Julius were both in their late teens, the similarities ended there. Frank was strong and handsome, Julius frail and gaunt with blemishes typical of a teenage boy.

Julius stood in front of me with his head down, infected tracks visible on his arms hanging from his shoulders like ropes. It was clear his addiction to heroin was ravaging his body and soul.

Julius wrapped his arms tightly around his trunk to embrace his screaming inner organs as he pleaded, "I want to go home; please take me home." But going home to Detroit was not an option because Julius was addicted to heroin, very sick, and too far away to make it back safely. While he was reeling and craving the drug—and *only* the drug, the relief of a hit was a universe away!

I couldn't believe Frank had been so careless as to bring him to the sticks with no plan or notification; he said it was a "last minute idea."

"We should take him to the hospital now before he gets really sick," I said.

"No," Julius replied, "no hospital, please." He was hunched over, looking down at the floor.

Paul was upstairs, and I felt very grateful that two of our babies were in bed, and the other two were in the upstairs playroom. The children were far away from the *mess of a situation* going on in the kitchen.

"It's dangerous for your brother—I really don't want the kids to see this, Frank," I said. "I want to help, but this is not the place for it, and I'm not the person."

"Yeah, I know," he said sheepishly. Frank threw out a possible option—"I know a preacher who has a place outside of town. He lives alone and he might let Julius stay with him for a couple of days."

I thought for a moment and then said, "It'll take more than a couple of days, but call your friend and see what he says." As Frank went into the other room to make the call, I tried to get Paul's attention from the bottom of the stairs in the dining room, but he didn't respond.

Frank returned with news that his preacher friend, John, was willing to have Julius come to his house. I was relieved there was a solution, but didn't think it was the best option. "You must know this isn't a good idea, Frank. You must've seen people in the throes of withdrawal."

Frank ignored my comment. "Will you come with us?" he asked.

For a moment I sat silent and then answered. "Frank, I don't like this; your brother is sick and he's going to get sicker. I need to talk to Paul first." I tried to solicit Paul's attention one more time; I yelled from the kitchen—"Honey, please come down."

Paul came around the corner. "What? What do you wan—"

When he saw the three of us, he stopped in mid-sentence. Julius was just a few feet from Paul, who could see immediately that something wasn't right.

"This is Frank's brother, Julius. He's sick and addicted to heroin and we're trying to talk him into going to the hospital.

Frank has a friend who'll let him come to his house, but Julius needs medical attention."

Paul attempted to use his powers of persuasion to convince Julius to go for medical help, but Julius wouldn't budge.

Without discussion Paul and I knew I'd be the one to go with Julius to the country house. I was a nurse, and Paul always abdicated when it came to medical matters or questions of the human spirit. So, out the door I went, leaving him to rally Lisa and Chris, who were five and six, and put them to bed. In those days men were conveniently incompetent when it came to household tasks. But jokingly I told Paul that his fancy, ivy league education and his two tours in Vietnam had prepared him to handle anything in a pinch.

Chapter Twenty-Four

Withdrawal

When Frank, Julius, and I arrived at the small country home, the preacher was waiting for us at the door. When he spotted Julius, he wore an Oh-my-God look on his face.

"This is John," Frank said, "the preacher I told you about." I shook the preacher's hand firmly, looked straight into his eyes, and said. "I don't know what would've happened if you hadn't agreed to this."

"Come in, come in." John was a young, pleasant-looking chap and it was evident that he was apprehensive as he invited us in.

"He really needs a hospital," I said.

"I agree," John said softly. "I can see he's very sick, but we can't drag him, and I'm not sure they'd take him if we did."

In that moment John and I became allies, his kindness reinforcing my faith in the inherent goodness of people.

Frank had a firm grip on his brother as he sat him down on the seasoned blond sofa at the edge of the living room. But, Julius couldn't stay seated. He periodically paced back and forth, his hunched body growing more and more contracted. At one point he pulled into a fetal position on the floor. We helped him to his feet and John got a paper bag in response to Julius's persistent gagging. When we got to the bathroom he began to retch and heave into the toilet. "I need to go home," he pleaded between episodes of vomiting green bile. "Please take me home." His body was shaking more violently, every cell of it craving the drug; but in this isolated area, there was none to be found.

Frank helplessly and quietly stood next to his brother as I made the plea. "Home is very far away, Julius," I said. "Let us help you; let us take you to the hospital."

He continued to refuse.

After several hours of agonizing withdrawal, Julius was a truly broken young man. But in spite of the horror he was experiencing, he showed no signs of anger. As a nurse I'd witnessed withdrawal and it was always accompanied by angry desperation. As he continued to ask to go home more insistently, I sensed a gentle and loving soul beneath the illness.

In the early morning hours, Julius developed a burning fever. His gaunt, ashen face turned to bronze. Worried that the infected track marks on his arms had poisoned his blood, I pulled Frank into the kitchen to convince him that we had only one option.

"Look, your brother's condition is very serious and I'm sure you don't want him to die out here. We're *all* responsible for him, now. Tell him the sickness will go away if he goes to the hospital. We're going to have to call an ambulance because there's no choice."

John agreed and said, "I'll call now."

"OK, OK." Frank said. "You tell him, though."

"I'll tell him," I said, as I left the kitchen, "but his response is irrelevant."

"Julius, you'll die without help. You've *got to go to the hospital.* You have a burning fever and you could have blood poisoning. Please trust me, this'll work for you. It can't get much worse than it already is. Please go willingly. It'll be better, I promise. Please trust me on this. Please trust me on this."

"OK, OK, I'll go." Julius finally caved in, and we all sighed in relief.

Shortly after John made the call an ambulance arrived with its lights flashing. Julius was moaning on the sofa when the EMTs came in. After assessing the situation, they wanted to get a stretcher. But Julius insisted he could walk. Reluctantly, they each took an arm and assisted him to a stretcher in back of the vehicle. They proceeded to lift him gently onto the cushion, laid him flat, and strapped him in securely.

Once he was in the cabin of the ambulance he began again, "I need to sit up. I need to sit up. I'm gonna throw up again." When the straps were released, Julius sat up instantly and began to gag, but there was nothing left in his stomach.

I agreed to travel in the ambulance with Julius. The local hospital had refused to take him, so we had a long, arduous ride to City Hospital an hour and a half away.

Julius was placed in a private room where he slept for several days. The hospital personnel administered medications to keep Julius tranquil and antibiotics to kill the infection. He slept until the poisons had been flushed out of his system. Medicine, clean sheets, and kind faces nurtured him out of his dependency and freed him of the tremors, nausea, and vomiting; antibiotics treated the infection and fever.

Paul and I never discussed Julius coming to live with us. It was understood that Frank would pick up his brother and bring him home.

Many of our friends said nothing about our decision to accept both young men into our home; we knew they thought we were making risky choices. But after Albion, we believed anything was possible. We really did *not* understand that Wynton and Albion were as different as any two places in America could be.

We settled Julius into the large room on the top floor with Frank. They appreciated the privacy and being away from the noise of little children squealing and carrying on. They always allowed the kids to play in their space when they were out of the house, or doing other things, and the young men proved to be worthy of the space. They were both immaculate and organized. I suspected their mother had influenced them in this regard.

Once when I was washing the floor, Julius commented on the smell of Pine Sol, and recalled his mother cleaning the bathroom. He and Frank said that she always did a great job. It was a small thing, but there was pride in their recollection, and I found it lovely.

From what they'd said I was left with impressions of a sad and overwhelmed woman who toiled in silence. Reportedly her life was steeped in generations of poverty, and my heart stirred at the young men's reflections of her. It was rare to find young men that age as neat and orderly as they were, and I'm sure their mother had taught well. While I never knew Frank and Julius's mother, I felt connected to her.

Julius quickly fell into the vibe of living with us, but unlike his brother, he seemed incredulous at his new life. He likened living with us to being in a soap opera; he thought people like us were only found on TV shows or in fairy tales. He hadn't seen a family eat dinner together, or a child spontaneously hugged. Even in the safety of our home he felt unsafe when his head hit the pillow at night. Perhaps he sensed something we didn't.

CHAPTER TWENTY-FIVE

Risks and Warnings

As our first politically liberal action, Paul and I created a George McGovern campaign center in our home with literature and plans in the making for a phone tree and such. When no one came to the center, we realized that local McGovern supporters were clearly in the minority. We'd been naïve about politics until then.

It became clear during that presidential election of 1972 that this was not a place that was going to embrace our newfound political liberalism. And we also learned that racism was still alive and well in America.

Paul and I never imagined we were living in a social powder keg. In this community life was characterized by hunting, drinking beer, and telling racist and anti-Semitic jokes. While the town must have had its share of good and benevolent people, we concluded that some harbored raw racist sentiments that hovered like a storm cloud contaminating the atmosphere. This town was not the best place for two young men of color to rise from the ashes.

Unfortunately, we didn't foresee that the lack of tolerance in town ran so deep, or that it would so profoundly affect the brothers. We hadn't anticipated hatred.

Frank was very good looking. I felt a warning was necessary. "This isn't Woodstock Frank, and the rest of the town isn't like Paul and me," I said.

I knew he'd dismissed my warnings as an overreaction, because, a couple of days later, he accidentally dropped a small packet with a condom in it on his way out the kitchen door. He clearly hadn't gotten my point.

When things were settled for Julius, as they had been for Frank, we wondered what the next step should be for us *and* for them. Neither Frank nor Julius had ever worked in legitimate jobs, so employment wasn't in their field of vision. They had lived at home with their mother and survived on the streets.

Paul's mission was to get them to move forward into their new lives, and he was firm. It's possible that Frank had answered the earlier newspaper ads by phone. Paul did all he could to convince them that they needed to fill out written job applications. Because Frank had already failed to find work, he was resistant to trying again. Neither Frank nor Julius was optimistic.

"You need to get a job, it's not realistic for you to go through life thinking of *manual labor* as a guy," Paul had said in jest. They laughed, but learned quickly that he was serious. While the act of looking for work seemed a simple task to *us*, it wasn't for *them*.

Frank could be very convincing, but he had bristled when he had to fill out applications asking about the year he had graduated from high school, his job history, and skill set. He couldn't confabulate his way to success; with concrete written questions he was at a loss. They both respectfully agreed to try, *in earnest*, to get jobs. It seemed apparent that they were trying to make Paul happy, and they did—by agreeing.

Though Frank was resistant, his energy and personality seemed conducive to the task. Julius, on the other hand, was docile and passive. He often sat quietly without expressing himself. He continued to appear depressed and troubled. While his infected arms had healed and his sunken cheeks had filled out, he lacked energy and enthusiasm—which didn't make him a compelling candidate for employment. Though Julius was born in contemporary America, he had been held neatly in place like the generations before him. While it was likely that his ancestors had been in bondage on plantations, the streets bound Julius, where survival had been the single goal for both him and his brother.

Days passed and each morning Frank and Julius came down for breakfast expecting that the day would be like the one before it, but hoping for more. I was always consumed with the children in the mornings. Julius and Frank were consumed with each other and trying to figure out what they would be doing on that day and in the future.

During breakfast Susan would occasionally catch Frank's attention, and he would casually gesture to her in the midst of a conversation. While neither brother was particularly attentive to the kids, we were all pretty comfortable with one another. For whatever reason, the kids gravitated toward Julius. He was always quietly thoughtful with them, and it was clear that Lisa, in particular, liked him better than his brother.

By afternoon the boys would be in and out of the house, lost sheep wandering on and off a pasture with no direction. Frank had made one local friend, a shy blue-eyed, blond boy named Tony.

I felt sorry for Tony. Whenever he was anxious, or shy, his face would turn bright red against his blond hair and blue eyes. I liked him, but he made me feel sad and sympathetic. Tony was a hypochondriac, and when he asked me about his many ailments, I gave him simple advice. Frank and Julius often referred to him as "No Cahone-Tony." I let them know it was cruel talk, but there was enough truth in it to make me chuckle.

CHAPTER TWENTY-SIX

More Surprises

Frank and Julius had little to do during the days. They stayed in their room for much of the time and Julius remained quietly depressed. He wore the mantle of a "victim," and it appeared that a meaningful life was a far reach for him; we realized that he had no expectations of a better life, because he didn't know he could live one. He was *perceived* as less smart, less beautiful, less human—less, less, and less! Survival was the best-perceived outcome.

After much prodding Frank and Julius hit the pavement. Frank's recovery network and our friends offered some job opportunities. They had to get up early to work at various odd jobs. As they were accustomed to sleeping in, we bought them an alarm clock. By the time the kids and I got down for breakfast, they had gone to work. Considering they'd never worked, they were consistent, competent, and did well in a variety of jobs including painting the inside of a local church and a couple of houses. They also cleaned yards. When the work ran out, the problems began.

To Paul and me, viable options were close at hand. "You have to get jobs; you need to get work and you can start again, now. Fill out applications, start calling," Paul insisted.

We soon realized that what might have been easy for people from our background was nearly impossible for two recovering addicts from the streets. There really *was* no work for Frank and Julius, not in *this* small town, anyway.

When Frank had come to live with us, he had a wardrobe. I think he had bought it during his drug days in Detroit where he had become accustomed to having his cloths dry-cleaned. While he had given up drugs, he never did give up this one extravagant pleasure. He was a classically good-looking young man, who enjoyed grooming his three-inch *Afro* and wearing his freshly dry-cleaned cloths with pride. While he was working in town he could pay the fees, buy gas, and insure his car. When the money dried up, and his bills accumulated, so did the pressure.

One day Frank said, "I think your kids deserve a new TV." A red flag went up. It was about the same time a TV had been reported missing from the church he and Julius had painted several weeks earlier.

When Frank and Julius realized that it wasn't going to be easy to sell the TV in this little town, they thought our kids should have it. As bizarre as it seems, they thought it was a way to pay us back while showing their appreciation and loyalty.

Paul and I knew the TV was stolen, and we were appalled. "You will never bring *that* TV into *this* house," we said, "and you need to figure out a way to put it back."

At first Frank was defensive, but then he said, "OK—we'll figure out a way to get it back." In their distorted thinking, they were attempting to be responsible, and in the absence of jobs, that meant paying their bills in any way possible.

A couple of months passed and the brothers continued to struggle without any opportunity for work. When I noticed an article in the local paper outlining the robbery of a jewelry store, I was highly suspicious!

The thieves had broken a display window and grabbed an $850 diamond ring. Though Frank remained congenial and Julius quiet and depressed, neither of them could look me in the eye.

In addition, Julius had come home with a gash in his leg. When I asked him about it, he cowered until Frank quickly stepped in and said he had gashed it on a piece of metal when they were in the junk yard looking for a part for his car. I was sure that he had injured his leg in reaching for the ring, but there was no proof. I drifted into "denial" and it kept my intuition in check with Paul's help. "You can't go around accusing people," Paul said. In my heart of hearts, I knew they had robbed the store. But Paul was comfortable in his denial.

Two weeks later, no news had surfaced about the robbery. Not long after this Julius began to show an interest in his trump card for success—art. He would often doodle and sketch as we sat at the dinner table, and I was impressed. I thought it might be good for him to try his hand at *real art*, so we bought him some paints as an early birthday present. He loved the gift and quickly immersed himself.

When Julius first began to paint, he would look at his work, analyze it, tweak it, and in the end he would say, "I think this might be pretty good."

It was, in fact, *very* good. Painting brought out a person that none of us had seen. His brain cells started to fire and at one point he gave me a small gift, a piece of art entitled "Because." And then he gifted me an oil of a mother and child. I was impressed with the paintings, so I called my friend, Jeanie, an art dealer and teacher, to ask her to review his work.

On a sunny day in early fall Jeanie came over, full of a vivacious enthusiasm. She put Julius at ease immediately, and the two of them went to his room on the third floor where he'd been painting. When the two of them descended from the attic I asked "How did it go?"

Jeanie smiled broadly and said, "It seems that Julius has talent!" She went on to talk about the quality of Julius's work and then she encouraged him to submit a portfolio through her to an art school.

Though there weren't a lot of pieces, it took several days to prepare his paintings. When his small portfolio was complete, Jeanie was eager to submit it to the art school in New York where she had been a part-time teacher.

Three days later Julius learned that the committee loved his work and subsequently offered him a full scholarship to attend the winter semester. Even his room and board would be covered.

The opportunity stunned him and the approval of his work had inspired a new confidence and sense of self-worth. It was a great thing to see him become aware of his own personal credibility. For the first time there was a skip in his step, and a smile on his face. Julius was no longer a monotone appendage of his brother; he stopped following Frank around like a wounded puppy.

A couple of weeks later, Julius offered to come to the grocery store to help me maneuver heavy bags. My back had been bothering me, so I appreciated the offer. I found his demeanor curiously subdued for the entire ride to the market, but assumed he was tired.

When we reached the grocery store he grabbed a cart, and followed me in. We meandered through the aisles as I filled the basket. Julius helped to fill several brown bags as the cashier tallied up the order. He was being particularly helpful and as we left the grocery store, he navigated the heavy cart along ahead of me until he was in the middle of the parking lot where he stopped for no apparent reason.

I caught up with him. He was standing still and looking down at his shoes, as he had been on the first night I met him. Out of *the blue* he said, "You must think the guys who robbed the jewelry store are really bad!"

There was a compelling shame and intensity in his voice. We were face to face when he lifted his head and looked directly into my eyes in a way that said, "I'm so, so sorry." I stood motionless knowing I'd been correct in my earlier assumptions; now there was no denying Frank and Julius had indeed taken the diamond ring from the jewelry store.

After Paul had pressured them to find a way to pay their bills, Frank and Julius did their best to find work, but to no avail. As distorted as it was, for them robbing the jewelry store was a way to meet Paul's expectations. It had become apparent that we'd underestimated the challenges.

My eyes filled with tears. *Julius is a different person at this point,* I thought, *what possible good could come of a jail sentence?* I quickly began to build a defense for my young friend in justifying the crime: *the jewelry store is heavily insured and there were no physical injuries.*

In admitting guilt in the midst of success, Julius had disarmingly revealed remorse. While he *wanted* to be an artist, he *needed* to be honest, to own up to the new standards of loyalty and responsibility that we'd defined for him. Surely, his mother had laid that foundation.

It was *Paul and my* turn to define the parameters of right and wrong, now cloudy to *me*. I had no idea what to do. I was ambivalent, confused, and very aware of the potential for Julius to become a user again. Julius was on the edge of a new life. Getting caught would have made his situation more than precarious.

He anxiously waited for my response. When he saw the stream of tears on my face, he too was at a loss. A truck approached and we were both relieved to be forced to move swiftly to my car. We remained silent as he lifted my groceries into the trunk.

Less than ten years separated Julius and me, but I had grown to feel like his mother, or more appropriately, like a "parentified" older sister. Perhaps this further inspired me to deny the seriousness of the robbery. I was caught between common values and reality, and there was no obvious way to escape.

On the ride home I didn't know what to *feel*, so I willed myself to stop feeling. I didn't know what to *do*, so I did *nothing*! If the truth about the robbery were to come out, Julius would be faced with new challenges, but for now he would be allowed to keep his dream. As I drove home I decided I would never be the one to take hope from Julius.

Paul and I knew that Julius's world had changed; he clearly understood what was expected of him. His remorse had been enough to cause me to look the other way and to keep us silent.

Julius began to thrive in our forgiveness. He had talent, a good heart, and now he had the possibility and the desire to succeed in a way he'd never before imagined. Discovering and expressing his talent had provided him with a new identity. Trading addict for artist—he was now worth more than a heroin fix.

But, as Julius came into his *own*, Frank became threatened and continued to operate according to *his* definition of loyalty. His flamboyant display of it made Paul and me nervous, and we realized that anyone who said or did anything to hurt us or our children, could face his wrath. It was as if he was trying to get our approval in the face of his brother's success.

I became convinced that Frank's interpretation of my silence relative to the jewelry store was different from Julius's. Because Julius had been honest with me, I looked the other way. It was likely that Frank perceived my behavior as an indication of unconditional acceptance of *his* actions. In this case, acceptance was complex and a serious problem.

The solution was not apparent. The assumption was that if one brother got legally charged with the crime, the other would follow as a result of it. So, my decision to protect Julius left Frank unaccountable. In keeping the issue of the robbery quiet, I had become complicit in crime, but I still chose to stay silent. In retrospect, I had no choice, because when it came to Julius, *family loyalty was family loyalty.*

In Julius's new frame of mind he felt free to move on with an appreciation and respect for the opportunity he had been given and he was elated as he made plans to leave for art school after Christmas.

On the streets of Detroit, Frank had been a leader, an identity that had taken him one step above an addict. In the *hood* he was the exception rather than the rule, a hustler among victims. His confidence had allowed him to move from the streets to rehab. We came to see that being at the center of the world was Frank's *goal* and he did everything he could to stay there. Frank was musically talented and his vanity motivated him to always look his best. With his charm and masculinity came a *bella figura*[12] that facilitated instant acceptance. In many ways, Frank could be described as having the skills of a quintessential con artist.

---

12 *Bella Figura*: In Italy this is a common description for a person with a fine appearance, and an ability to impress others.

Because Frank was being pressured to pay for his car and his excessive dry cleaning bills, it's likely he had masterminded the TV and jewelry store thefts to that end and that Julius had acted out of loyalty to his brother in both crimes. Before the art scholarship, Julius was at Frank's beck and call, and Frank would have accepted nothing less. Frank "knew" he had saved his brother, and that meant Julius would be beholden to him forever.

Frank became increasingly intimidated by his brother's happiness and positive identity. The fact that Julius savored the promise of a new future drove Frank to escalate. I began to question his mental status; his shenanigans would prove to be catastrophic.

After dinner one night Susan was following me around the kitchen trying to get my attention. I was distracted because Frank and I had had words. He was about to run off with his friend Tony to play pool at the Wynton Pub on the outskirts of town. Julius had left earlier which had aggravated Frank, who was not used to having his brother be so independent.

The bar was a watering hole where townies gathered to drink, play pool, and commiserate. I was sure the clientele wouldn't be happy to see Frank and Julius at the pub. The demographics of the establishment were white, white, and white; the appearance of any person of color was an aberration. Again, *power* in this small remote town was fueled with guns, drinking beer, and telling racist jokes. The pub attracted *power*.

Frank's considerable charm had been well received by many of our friends, and by those who helped him through his struggle with heroin, but his strength could easily be a liability in the face of overt racism. In his current state of mind, there was even more reason to worry. He had no perception of the extent of the danger and neither did we. I tried to convince him to reconsider his plan to meet Julius and their only local friend, Tony, but he was bent on going, and grew more agitated with every word.

Because Julius was less likely to pose a threat to the white guys in the bar, I wasn't as concerned about him being there at that point. Julius was not motivated to "outshine" a local, or to "hook up" with a woman. In some ways, he knew better. Tony would let the patrons know that Julius was OK; people in Wynton respected veterans, and Tony had recently returned from Vietnam.

As I tried my best to persuade Frank, I noticed a strap across his chest and a bulge in his jacket. I couldn't see it, but I *knew* it was a gun. I was afraid to confront him because of his agitated state of mind. It was almost as if he intended for me to "see" the weapon, but then changed his mind. He abruptly turned and pulled his blazer lapel close to his chest as he walked through the small ironing room and into the office on the street side of the house where his car was parked.

When he was barely out of sight, I realized Susan had left the room and I didn't know where she was. I immediately followed in Frank's direction, and as I entered the office, I saw him squatting down on one knee while chastising Susan. "You're being bad . . . you shouldn't be in here. Your mother doesn't want you in here!" he said, as he looked directly into Susan's face. I felt a burst of terror that a gun could be so close to my child.

Frank's hands on her shoulders, Susan stood motionless, seeing anger in his face for the first time. Susan sensed his rage and I could tell she was afraid.

I was aware how important it was to keep my wits about me at that moment and was very careful in my response. "You need to apologize to Frank, honey." I said.

Frank was taken aback; he stopped short when Susan apologized. At a loss as to where he should next place his anger, he rose to his feet and said, "I'm leaving."

As the door slammed behind him I took a deep breath. I was relieved he was out of the house, but suspected there was more to come. *This is not OK. He's going to find trouble out there tonight.*

When Frank was gone, I hugged Susan. "You're a good girl, honey," I said, "but you can't run off without telling Mommy where you're going."

"But Mommy, I just went away for a minute."

I had acted intuitively—how could a small child have understood the complexity of the situation? When Susan went into the other room, it was neither unusual nor significant, but I had chastised her to divert Frank.

The potential for things to go wrong weighed on me. Hope escaped me in the absence of trust. *The rednecks and I— we're all reckless in different ways.*

I felt profoundly guilty, stupid, and afraid. I made one non-negotiable decision—Frank had to go. I grabbed Susan, and as I carried her upstairs, I thought—*I'll put the kids to bed and then talk to Paul, they need to be in bed before I can deal with this.*

Children bounce back in minutes—the incident had been but a blip in Susan's day. As I climbed the stairs, I sang a little song my father had written for the kids.

> She is a putza kid, a putza kid, a putza kid.
> She is a putza kid, on a sunny day—YAY!

She giggled and hugged me, and when we reached the top stair, she ran to find her sister and brother. She squealed, and for a brief moment I was afraid she'd wake up Baby Joanie as she ran by her door.

In the playroom on the second floor, Paul was sitting on the sofa reading as Lisa and Chris acted out a fantasy action adventure on either side of him. Paul could remain focused, even when kids crawled all over him. They were bickering over who would play the hero as Paul read his book. I would talk things over with him when I got the kids to bed so we could talk in peace.

As Paul sat undisturbed, I guided Lisa, Christopher, and Susan to the bathroom. I filled the tub with warm water as the girls scurried out of their clothes. Lisa and Susan went into the water first, and when they were clean, I wrapped them in towels. I felt my stomach knot as I dried my dripping daughters. Chris followed.

My thoughts were racing. *Should I call the police? What did Frank intend to do with the gun? What if the bulge in his pocket isn't a gun? What if he's already sold the gun by the time the police get there?*

After the children were tucked in, I went downstairs to turn off the lights. In my exhaustion, I dropped onto the seat of the living room sofa. I wanted the nausea to go away, so I took a couple of deep breaths as I closed my eyes to calm myself. The living room, with its celery colored walls and dimmed lights, was a great place to ponder, but my mind wouldn't quiet.

I should've gone upstairs to talk to Paul, but I chose to sit for a *long* time and ruminate over possible solutions. In the end, I had no viable answers.

Finally, I got up from the seat and turned the lights off. *A shower will clear my mind.*

I relished the flow of the hot running water and as it hit the back of my neck, the tension eased. When it was over, I dried myself off, slipped into my robe, and tip-toed down the long hall to our bedroom.

By this time it was eleven o'clock. Paul was often called back to the plant to deal with a crisis, so he was rarely asleep at this time of night, and when he was home, he stayed up and read. But tonight, he was in a deep sleep. I crawled gently under the covers so as not to disturb him. *Now what should I do?*

I decided to let Paul sleep. Perhaps I had procrastinated on purpose, for fear he would react in a way that would make the situation worse—perhaps.

As usual, Paul had left the light on and had dozed off while reading. I reached over my pillow to the switch, and turned it off. The moonlight showed through the huge bay window. I lay, quietly troubled, while looking lovingly at my sleeping husband. The rose of the walls softened the moonlight on his face and he looked particularly handsome. In the absence of answers, I distracted myself with midnight musings of *"how we came to be."*

Chapter Twenty-Seven

Distraction

I'd been attracted to Paul long before his intervention in my born-again experience, and long before he invited me to come to Harvard with my friends. I have a clear image of him walking down the hall of our Junior High School with his goop-backed hair and black leather jacket. I was a cheerleader in middle school, and ironically had *his* name to cheer about:

> Pimentel, Pimentel! He's our man.
> If he can't do it, no one can.

Paul was taller than most of the other boys, and good looking. In spite of his mother's efforts to hide a pink and black *Elvis Presley* shirt in the laundry, he wore it often. It was the '50s and every guy wanted to look like Elvis.

Paul now says he was first attracted to my face, but admits when challenged, that it was my full breasts that first caught his attention. Mine developed a little earlier than most girls my age, and he was thirteen. I had no idea of Paul's shallow attraction to me and he didn't realize that I found him attractive, either.

In spite of our initial impressions, we would not *be*. Paul was my good friend's boyfriend, and I was the smitten girl friend of the most sought-after guy in town. So we remained good friends on separate paths; while we found ourselves in the same circles, neither of us entertained any thoughts of a relationship.

When Paul and his girlfriend of many years broke up, he was miserable. He needed distraction, so I arranged for my friend Mary to go out with him. This was a really bad idea, as she was troubled and he was immature.

In high school Paul defied all stereotypes. He was a football nerd whose often exasperated coach would say, "You're the only idiot I know with a high IQ."

People liked Paul; he was the President of our 1960 high school graduating class. To fulfill his dream of joining the Navy to see the world, he joined the *Naval Reserves* in high school so as to go on active duty with seniority when he graduated. But his father wanted him to go to college and become President of the United States. Paul applied to Harvard expecting to be rejected. His plan was foiled when he was accepted and given a scholarship.

His dysfunctional relationship with Mary continued through high school graduation and into his first year at college, but it wasn't working.

Before my *born-again* boy friend, I had left my *off-and-on-again* boy friend of many years, because he had proven to be less than trustworthy. In my new freedom, I accepted Paul's invitation to bring a few of my friends from nursing school to a party at his dormitory. We both viewed the invitation to be one of friendship, so as not to betray his girlfriend. I wasn't going to be with him specifically, it was a *group thing*.

At Harvard the dorms are called houses and students share suites. When we entered the Eliot House living room we were greeted, then offered glasses of a dry ice concoction from a punch bowl on a small table in the middle of the room. Mist poured over its edges, so we chose not to partake of the brew for fear it would kill us. The boys were very disappointed. The only other refreshment was a sparse amount of pretzels and chips. Rock 'n' roll blared from speakers.

Later, as we drove down Storrow Drive in Boston, we talked about the silly Harvard boys and wondered if they thought they were smarter than a group of student nurses. We knew the dry ice concoction and a few snacks were part of an evil plot and contrived with great expectation—and it wasn't going to happen. Chatter ensued about Paul and his feelings for me. "It's so obvious that he loves you, can't you see it?"

"He's my friend's boyfriend. Paul and I have been friends for years," I said. "You're *way* off the mark."

My friend Claire chimed in, "She may be his girl, but the fact is, he has an eye for *you*."

"Well you're all just crazy, there's no future in it," I said, "and besides, I could never—a friend is a friend, so just stop it!"

It didn't take long for Paul's relationship with Mary to plummet into oblivion, and for his grades to do the same. In just one year he had gone from an honor student with all As, to being on the edge with all Ds. The university told him that he was having "a momentary lapse," and forced him to take a year off. It was then that he sabotaged my relationship with the *born again* Texan Bob Marsh and with the cult I had taken up with. It was also when he told me he loved me for the first time.

I was thankful he decided to go back to college and become a more serious student again.

All that musing about what had been allowed me to drift off.

CHAPTER TWENTY-EIGHT

The Beginning of the End

I had been asleep only for a short time when the ringing phone startled me. I reached over to the far side of the nightstand to answer it. At first I was in a fog, but then I began to comprehend that Frank was rambling, his voice desperate.

"I'm shot! My arm is shattered and I think Julius is dead. They shot him in the back—in the *back*! I tried to give up. But they kept shooting and shooting. I'm bleeding. They're chasin' me. There's a bunch of guys, maybe seven of them. They have lots of guns and they're trying to kill me, too!"

"Oh, my God," I blurted.

"What is it?" Paul asked, half asleep.

Frank went on. "I'm in the phone booth near the woods, you know the one. It's on the left as you're driving away from town."

"I know the one. Frank, stop talking and find a place to hide."

When I hung up, I immediately told Paul I was leaving and to call the police and tell them there'd been a shooting at the phone booth on the way out of town.

Paul asked again in a sleepy voice, "What's happening?"

"Julius and Frank have been shot. We'll talk later."

I left Paul in bed, confused—and like me—unable to fathom what he was hearing. With no awareness of the events of the early evening, he had no idea what was going on.

I *should have called the police earlier; I should have called them!*

I quickly put on a pair of jeans and headed for the door.

"Where are you going?" Paul asked.

"To meet the police at the phone booth," I said, as I headed out the door.

Dazed and half asleep, he didn't try to stop me. He was usually the boss. But, in times like these, he trusted me. Paul had an ultimate faith in my instincts—too *much* faith. So, he left Frank and Julius in my domain on that tragic night.

As I drove in the darkness I was emotionally paralyzed, but intent on staying in control. *Maybe Julius is alive, maybe Frank's wrong.* I headed for the phone booth intent on making sure the police arrived first.

I couldn't deal with Julius's demise in the midst of a tempest. Denial could hold my feelings in check for just so long. For a brief moment, reality crept in. *If I had called the police, Julius might still be alive.*

Just when the heater in my car began to pump warm air, I spotted a cruiser with blinking lights in the distance. An ambulance with a blaring siren approached from behind. I pulled over and allowed it to join the police cars before I followed it to its destination.

It was as if everything had been perfectly synchronized. When I pulled up behind the ambulance, I spotted Frank moving sheepishly from his hiding place near the phone booth. His demeanor was markedly changed from when he'd left the house. With cops milling around, Frank walked toward me.

Frank stayed close to me as he held his arm in pain—a frightened baby trying to hide in the folds of his mother's apron. His dry-cleaned clothes were bloodied and his perfectly groomed afro had become matted in his desperate attempt to hide in the woods. As he looked for my support, I said nothing. I guided him to the ambulance as he walked with intent and in relative safety.

From amid the chaos around the ambulance, a police officer started to help Frank into the ambulance. I quietly asked, "Have you frisked him for a gun?" The bulge in Frank's jacket before he left the house had become impossible to deny. Frank heard my request, but showed no emotion, and remained contrite. I had no personal fear of him in the moment, but feared that the weapon could be carelessly discharged in the ambulance.

The police officer reached into Frank's jacket and pulled out the revolver. Frank remained silent, resigned to his fate.

I joined him in the ambulance. My profound disappointment was palpable. Frank knew his opportunity for a better life had vanished in the events of the night and in his unconscionable choices.

I made perfunctory and superficial comments to ease the tension as the ambulance sped along. "It's a short ride to the hospital. It won't be long now."

I felt many things all at once. Along with anger, sadness, and betrayal, I also felt a profound relief that Frank would never live with my family again; he had closed that door.

When we entered the Emergency Room hallway, the paramedics took Frank into a treatment room. In a short time a nurse emerged, and I heard her tell a policeman that Frank was being prepped for surgery to remove the bullet and repair the bones in his elbow. She then said, "His brother is in serious condition."

Julius is still alive—I heard her say it—he's alive!

I was able to get the nurse's attention for a moment, "I'm a friend of Julius's. *Is* he alive?"

"He's fighting for his life, but he *is* still alive," she said, as she rushed back to her work.

Learning that Julius was alive, I felt little relief, no catharsis of emotion. Beyond a small glimmer of hope, I felt nothing. We were in the middle of a nightmare. I wondered if Julius would have ever gotten here if I had called the police.

I needed to hear Paul's voice, so I called him from a phone booth. He answered quickly. "Where are you?"

I gave him the details. He was shocked and relieved that I was at the hospital and not out beside the road. He had called the police, but had no information.

"What now?" he asked.

"I don't know, honey, but I'll wait until it feels right to leave. Can you handle the kids?"

"Sure. Just keep me posted."

I found my way back to a bench in the emergency room. I sat quietly and tried to distract myself by taking note of the various police officers and characters milling around. One of the local policemen had a big belly that covered his belt, and when he leaned over to pick up a pack of cigarettes that had slipped from his fingers, his pants fell well below the crack of his ass. He quickly hauled them up.

As he lifted his head we locked eyes for a brief second, and it wasn't pleasant for either of us. There was a chill in his stare. Maybe he thought I was Frank's girlfriend or partner in crime, but it could just have easily been a projection of my emotion. I wished that Paul was with me to set the record straight; people rarely questioned Paul. He had a strong presence and confidence that was seldom misinterpreted.

I began to shiver. *This is really complicated. I need to get it together.*

The officials and medical staff continued to chatter across the hall. After a while I got up enough nerve to approach the officer who had inadvertently displayed his butt. My intention was not only to learn more, but also to hold my ground with him.

"Have you any news about Julius's condition?" I asked. He paused for an extraordinarily long time before he raised his eyebrows, and looked away. No answer. I asked again. "Well, *have* you?"

He cocked his head like a parrot. "Yeah. He's barely alive," he said with a belligerent glare.

I went back to my seat and lifted my head high so as not to give him the power of intimidation; I wondered how often men like Julius had been treated with the same contempt.

Eventually, I got the attention of a nurse who was running down the hall. "Yes, how can I help you?" she asked.

"Please keep me posted on what's happening with Julius—he lives with us," I replied. She gently touched my arm and said, "I'll let the doctor know," bringing subtle warmth and comfort to the icy room.

When I returned to my seat this time, a state trooper in plain-clothes sat next to me. He was inscrutable, but he had a professional approach; I wanted to be honest with him at all costs, but was apprehensive about his inquisition. After answering several questions about how I knew Frank and Julius, he got specific.

"Do you know where Frank got the gun?"

I was squirming; I wasn't sure of how to respond. I didn't know where the gun had come from. But I had alerted the local police to its existence out at the phone booth.

In Wynton, securing a gun wasn't difficult. I suspected that Tony had gotten it for Frank, or at the very least, knew where it came from. "Have you asked his friend Tony?" I asked. The officer took note.

Just then Tony popped into the dimly lighted hallway. "There's Tony," I said, pointing at the nice-looking young man entering the room. He spotted me and waved.

The officer left my side and walked over to question Tony, but I couldn't hear them.

I wondered, *"Could they have teased Tony at the pub, and caused a riff that resulted in the shootings?"* Two black guys demeaning a local, white veteran would have been enough to set things off.

After the interview with the state trooper, activity increased. Nurses scurried in and out of the *ER* treatment room where Julius was struggling for his life. In a hospital this size there was only one emergency room doctor, who'd been in with Julius since my arrival.

As I sat outside the emergency room, I thought about my father, and was grateful he wasn't nearby. My parents had never met Frank and Julius, but I knew they would've been horrified that I was in this situation. It wasn't as if my father would've avoided a drama like this. He had, after all, primed me to be a reckless risk taker. But he was also an old-fashioned guy who believed that women needed to be protected and in their place. *He can never know this story*, I told myself—*never*!

Finally a nurse invited me into the room where Julius was being treated. "He wants to see you," she said.

Julius lay flat on the table with lots of lines and tubes in him. His breathing was labored and shallow and his face looked as ashen as it had when he'd arrived at our house that first night. Bullets or shrapnel had collapsed a lung, so they had thrust a large chest tube into the pleural cavity to create a vacuum; a large suction tube hung from the right side of his chest to equalize the pressure of the collapsed lung. This scene was all too familiar. The doctor had elevated the bottom of the *ER* table to help maintain Julius's blood pressure, and to address shock.

The attending physician had a kindness about him, and I was impressed with his sophistication and competence. I knew he was appalled by the havoc that had been visited on Julius. The young doctor quietly mumbled as he adjusted lines and tubes, "This is an abomination—an outrage!"

I moved to where Julius lay still and barely conscious. He opened his eyes but remained silent—I was no longer in denial.

"We need to move him now," the doctor said. "This hospital is ill-equipped to deal with his extensive injuries. He needs to be in Brookton. We don't do thoracic surgery here, and he needs an operation to stop the bleeding, and to remove bullets and extensive shrapnel. I'm in a quandary. He may *not* survive the trip, but he will *certainly* die if he stays here."

After I called Paul with another update, I moved swiftly into the cabin of the ambulance at the doctor's request. Julius's ghost-like face looked like those I'd seen in the morgue. But the transfer to the ambulance caused him to groan in pain, assuring me there was still life in his perforated body.

The nightmare continued as we sped through the darkness in the early morning mist, the red lights of the ambulance rotating. This was my second trip with Julius to Brookton in the early hours—once again fighting for his life. With his eyes at half-mast, he looked at me for one brief moment, and whispered, "Wouldn't it be something if I upped and died right now?" My eyes filled as they had in the parking lot of the supermarket on the day of his confession.

"You won't die," I replied in a whisper, but he wasn't awake to hear me.

When we arrived at Brookton, a surgical team was waiting. Without a word a nurse and anesthesiologist pushed Julius's stretcher toward the operating room.

More than three hours later a surgeon with bloody clothes and a used mask around his neck moved toward me across the waiting room, "He's in intensive care. I expect him to be there for a while. We removed a lot of shrapnel, and several bullets from his back, abdomen, and one bullet from his leg. We got most of it out, but there's a bullet lodged near his aorta that I was afraid to go after for fear of a rupture. It's a miracle he lived through this; he's a pretty strong kid."

Apparently, the good food and rehabilitation at our house had helped Julius survive the surgery; I allowed myself a small degree of satisfaction in knowing his health could have helped save him. I was totally exhausted by the time I called Paul. As Julius was stable and his survival was probable, I asked Paul to pick me up. By this time it was 9 A.M.

Fortunately it was a weekend when our friends, Judy and Cliff, could watch the kids. They had brought their children with them to our house, and when we got home, the kids were having fun playing together.

On Sunday morning Paul and I took the kids with us to Brookton, and we took turns visiting Julius while the kids played in the waiting area. We didn't want to bother Cliff and Judy again, and it gave us time together in the car and at the hospital. We arrived back home at about five, and I got the kids to bed early after the long and arduous day.

During the following few days Frank stayed in the local Wynton hospital to recover from the surgery on his shattered arm. At this point he was probably happy for the protection.

I later learned that Frank had been fortunate to have survived the mob. He'd held up a white handkerchief in surrender, but the shooters kept discharging their guns again and again and again.

The "hunters" only gave up the chase because of a pre-occupation with Julius, who had been shot to the ground.

At about nine o'clock on Tuesday night the phone rang. A soft male voice said, "Is this Sandy?"

"Yes, yes, it is. Who's this?"

"My name is Roland. I'm Frank and Julius's brother. I'm calling from a phone booth. We're all driving to the hospital from Detroit to see Julius. My mother is with us."

"I'm sure he'll be happy to see you all, particularly your mother."

Slowly and quietly, Roland said, "Yeah—I know. I wanna see Frank, too. Do you know where he is?"

"Well, he got shot in the elbow and had surgery. I think he's in a mental hospital now. He wasn't thinking clearly when all this happened. I guess the judge wanted to see what's going on in his head. But when he's discharged, he'll probably be going to jail to await trial. He was in the jail across from our house for a while, but he's not there anymore. I'm mad at Frank, Roland. I'm afraid he precipitated much of this. I don't know what he's done, but whatever it is, they've arrested him for it. He left the house with a gun, and I think that the shootings could've been avoided."

"I'm sorry," Roland said, "I don't know what happened or what's going on."

"For the most part, we don't know either. We can't figure out what's happening with the guys that shot your brothers—it's hard for us to understand that some of them are free and walking around. Justice is not commonplace here."

"OK," Roland said, "we're drivin' now, we'll see Julius tonight."

Late on the following Tuesday night the entourage from Detroit arrived at the hospital to visit Julius. They stayed for only a few hours before turning around and going back, so we never met them. Roland stayed behind to be with Julius.

I'd been away from my children more than I wanted to, so we chose to stay home for a couple of days and let Julius visit with Roland. I needed to be with my children.

Two days later I visited the hospital and found Roland by Julius's side; Julius was noticeably improved. It was good that he had seen his mother on Sunday, and he seemed happy to have his brother staying with him. The color had returned to his face and his voice was stronger. I wondered if he knew that he would have to live with a bullet next to his heart.

Roland offered me a chair next to Julius, and left to get coffee. Julius was happy to see me and glad to be alive. He began to chat in a whisper, "Roland doesn't understand us, he's thinking like I did when I first came. I didn't think that lives like yours were real—remember?"

"Yes, I *do* remember, Julius."

He continued, "Roland thought at first that you and I—well, you know. He didn't know how things could be, just like I didn't know. I didn't think people could care, unless there were reasons like, like—well it's hard for me to explain."

I looked at Julius with tenderness, realizing that in his sad short life, he'd learned only a few recent lessons to sustain him. Though he couldn't articulate it, he was talking about believing in life and seeing motives beyond sex, money, or drugs.

A nurse walked into the room. "Julius, we want you to walk. It's important."

"Really? I hurt *bad* everywhere."

"I know, Julius, but you need to move," the nurse said in a soft, but deliberate voice.

I excused myself to let the nurse do her work. As I stood in the hall, waiting for them to finish, I realized Julius was holding onto his new perception of life, in spite of the fact that he'd been shot in the back by people who were reportedly proud of their crimes.

When the nurse left the room, I went back in and sat next to Julius's bed.

Julius started—"I told Roland how it is with you guys, because I didn't want him to think things were different—he needed to know."

"Yes, I understand."

"He's going home when I leave here, but he's tired. He looks like I used to look—don't you think?"

"He does remind me of you, Julius."

"I hate to ask, but do you think he could stay upstairs for a couple of days? He can't get back to Detroit until the weekend."

We hadn't talked about the next step, and hadn't thought beyond the moment. I didn't know what was going to happen, but I said, "I'll need to talk to Paul. In light of what happened I'm nervous about having your brother stay with us—even for a few days."

"OK," Julius said, "OK, I understand."

Roland didn't look anything like Julius, but he was gentle and tentative in the same way Julius had been after detox. When he returned from the cafeteria, I told him I would call Paul and ask if he could come home with me. "We've been through a lot, Roland."

Julius had said that Roland was drug free and that he could be trusted. We gave in, but made it clear that Roland could only stay for two days.

"Thank you," Roland said in a soft voice, "I appreciate it."

Visiting hours were over, and it was an awkward walk to the car. Roland was shy and there was not a lot for us to talk about at that point. I commented on how quickly Julius was recovering in his drug-free and nourished condition.

"Yeah."

As I drove home, I pointedly said, "Julius told me you've had problems with drugs like him."

"Yeah, I was on drugs too, but no more."

"How'd you get clean?"

He put his face into his palms and thought for a moment. "I don't remember a lot of it, but it was about six months ago."

"Do you remember where you were?"

"It was some kinda camp somewhere. I remember the yelling, everything I said or did was wrong; no matter what I tried to do, they didn't like it. People were . . ." he stopped for a moment, "mean . . . they were mean."

"When you say *mean,* what did they do, Roland?"

"I don't know—they didn't whip me or anything like that." He paused. "I was alone for a long time, but then I was in a group. A guy kept yelling. 'You're *nothing,* a worthless piece of—well you know.' They shaved my head and made me stand without any clothes on."

Again, he cupped his face in his hands, and then he rubbed his cheeks with his palms. "I really don't wanna talk about it, I'm sorry. I just hate thinking about it. It was hard, I remember it being bad."

"How did you get there—what did you do?"

"It was *there—or* jail. I wish I had picked jail."

"How did you get in trouble in the first place?" I asked gently.

"A robbery, it was a robbery; another guy and I robbed a store to get money for drugs and I got caught; I wish I didn't do it—I don't need drugs, now."

Roland showed no evidence of anger, but the aftermath of trauma *was* evident; he exuded a palpable sadness—another casualty of the streets.

"What do you want to happen, now?" I asked.

"I don't know, to stay alive I guess, and out of jail."

His demeanor of brokenness was so much like Julius's when he'd first arrived. Roland was clearly not a *Frank.* Perhaps that's the reason we took him home with us.

The next day at about noon, the same state trooper who had interviewed Tony and me in the emergency room at Brookton Hospital paid us a visit. He'd been the only law enforcement person who presented as a professional—I liked him.

He was perfunctory when he asked if Roland was there.

"Yes," I said. "Come on in."

He softened with my greeting. "Can you bring me to him?"

"Come with me," I answered. *Here we go again. What now?*

The trooper and I walked together to the third floor. I knocked on the door at the bottom of the attic stairs, then called, "Roland, we need to talk to you, we're coming up."

When we reached the top step, Roland was standing quietly resigned as the state trooper identified himself.

"You're in violation of parole—please come with me."

"OK."

As the two of them headed for the door, Roland looked back and said, "Sorry, Sandy, and thank you." He was *that* matter of fact; he must have known it was coming.

The following day Roland's arrest was featured on the front page of the local newspaper.

The negative energy in Wynton was like smog, and I wondered how we'd ever landed in such a place. A wooden cross a little larger than a child's hand-held pinwheel had been burned on our lawn in the middle of the night. We didn't trust the local police at that point, so we didn't report it. Our crushed naïveté exposed our vulnerability, and for the first time, we feared for our family.

Cliff and Judy were the only ones we told about the cross. They'd been awakened to the dangers of Wynton before we were; when Cliff had fired a disgruntled employee, his life had been threatened in an offhand way at the plant. Cliff had been invited by the fellow to go hunting with his friends who said, "Some of us won't come back."

Cliff might have dismissed the comment as a bravado gesture, but a man who had worked for him had disappeared without a trace. Cliff had been told that the guy had offered drugs to the daughter of a local.

When the article in the local paper featured Roland's arrest, Charles, the plant manager, took Paul into his office and asked "What's going on over there? Maybe it's time for you to leave this to the professionals." We had great respect for Charles. He was a Christian role model, an Episcopalian *who walked the talk.*

Charles had been very supportive through all that had happened, but even he had his limits. Paul assured him he understood, and that our names wouldn't ever be on the front page of the newspaper again. Miraculously, Charles believed him.

We soon learned that we were under investigation and that our phone lines were being tapped. It didn't matter because we weren't saying or doing anything of any legal consequence. In some ways we were comforted by the fact that the police would be more apt to find the truth. We heard rumors that we had an FBI file, and that they were involved in the investigation.

Subsequently, the same state trooper came to our house to ask us questions, and it was obvious he'd figured out by then that we were innocent people who had no idea what we were doing.

"Did you find any drugs in the house?" the trooper asked.

"We haven't looked. Do you want to go through their stuff?"

"No," the officer said, "you look and if you find anything, let me know."

We later realized that the investigator was trying to protect us from ourselves; had he searched and found anything of consequence, Paul and I would have been implicated in a drug crime. We didn't find anything.

Through everything that happened in Wynton, Paul never flinched. He went to his job at the factory as he'd always done.

Virtually all of our friends stuck by us—even those from the Deep South who viewed things differently. Those who thought we were in over our heads were right. It was in Wynton that I realized that friendship means more than *being on the same page.*

Newspaper accounts of the shootings were sporadic and inconsistent. One said that Frank and Julius were having an argument over a pool game when Frank shot his brother in the leg.

Frank was charged with *intent to kill and pointing a deadly weapon.* It was reported later that the gun was never found. Since I had been the one to ask the police officer to take the gun on the night of mêlée, I found this curious. I surmised that the gun would have been found if the local police thought it would serve as evidence for Frank's conviction.

We weren't aware of any arrests when the local newspaper posted a surprising article on the front page. The reporter said that the town was well aware of the shootings that had occurred at the pub and referred to some who had been amused by the event. He further implied that those who were involved would be held accountable. Perhaps the article was in response to the rumors circulating about the shooters bragging about what they had done.

Paul and I were incensed that there'd been so few arrests. While we knew it was likely Frank had committed a crime, it was clear that he hadn't shot his brother multiple times in the back in cold blood. The fact that the police denied having confiscated his weapon was unnerving. So we called the NAACP in a nearby city and then a senator in Detroit to solicit his involvement. We weren't sure what had transpired, but we believed that Julius had been a victim. We heard nothing in response, but arrests were made shortly thereafter.

Later, the newspaper reported that on the night of the shootings the owner of the pub (who was also Justice of the Peace) and another patron were charged with *intent to commit murder, and pointing a deadly weapon.*

After recovering from surgery on his elbow, Frank left the local hospital. He was arraigned and put in jail in City Hall. I visited him to find out exactly what had happened. I didn't learn much. He did tell me that a state trooper had interviewed him and had asked if Paul was a drug dealer.

I was surprised when Frank laughed and said, "Are you kidding? Paul's too smart to deal drugs."

He wasn't alone in the cell. Ironically the patron who'd been charged with shooting him shared the same jail cell, and they were both acting friendly—it felt like old home week!

This was the only time I visited him—I was through.

Julius was discharged from the hospital without a word. It was likely he'd signed himself out against the doctor's advice and had gone back to Detroit. He left without a trace and never returned. Julius was clearly afraid to stay in town and we later learned that the jewelry store theft had come back to haunt him. Art school could no longer be a reality for Julius. It's likely he also felt responsible for Roland breaking parole.

Julius had left his paints and canvases on the third floor of our house along with his dream of going to art school. We hoped he'd learned enough to preserve his sobriety and potential for a better life—somewhere. We weren't optimistic, but nevertheless, Julius had talent, and we hoped.

A judge sent Frank away for a ninety-day psychiatric evaluation, and the men who'd been accused of shooting him and Julius were let out of jail on minimal bail.

While accepting that our association with Frank was over, we also felt he had the right to be fairly represented. So we asked Jim Wyman to represent him in court. He agreed to take it pro bono, and we were convinced he'd do his best to promote justice.

When Frank came back from his psychiatric evaluation, he stood trial for the jewelry theft. My friend Judy and I sat in the back of the court room, but I didn't think Frank knew I was there, and that was fine with me. I needed to know the truth; that would take years.

Attorney Wyman exchanged the breaking and entering charge for some kind of arrangement that would allow the Justice of the Peace and the patron to walk free as well. The extent of the theft was the $850 ring. The bottom line was that they all walked.

Shortly after his trial, Frank crossed the street and came to our back door. "I need to pick up my things," he said.

Frank appeared as he had on the first day we met him. A calm complacency had replaced his anger. I got the sense he felt lucky to be alive and free, and that he really didn't care that the men who had shot him and his brother were walking free as well.

My heart pounded in my chest in spite of his apparent improved state of mind. I wasn't afraid of him, but I knew I wanted him out of my house, and didn't want to have to spell it out for him.

I was relieved when Frank said, "I need to leave now and the judge said that Julius and I can't come back."

"Where's Julius?" I asked.

"I don't know. I haven't talked to him or anybody else, but I need my stuff." I had forgotten his cloths were in the attic.

"OK, just wait and I'll get them." He made no plea to get them himself.

I made two hikes to the attic to retrieve his belongings. I was happy that the kids were in school or taking naps when I retrieved several pair of pants, two jackets, and a number of shirts. Each had been neatly separated and put in plastic bags at the dry cleaners. I had tucked them away in an obscure part of the attic.

Frank said, "See ya," and off he went.

I didn't look out the window, but I heard a car drive away. He may have been transported to the bus station in a police cruiser. I really didn't care—I was just happy he was gone.

As I stood in my kitchen, I thought about the pathetic summary of Frank and Julius with sadness—and with relief that it was over for all of us. The only redemption in this sad story was that both young men had remained drug free.

While I came to believe that Frank would continue to try to manipulate life to his advantage, he now knew that being addicted would only disable him in his quest to get what he wanted.

Julius had had a glimpse of something beyond the streets, and had found something in himself beyond the desire to get high. Getting caught up in thoughts of, "What if . . ." only served to deepen my sadness.

A month or so after Frank left my kitchen, I received the call I needed to help me put my life back into perspective. To help me distance myself from the experience, I needed to feel something—anything—positive.

I was standing in our kitchen in Wynton in the spring of 1973 when my good friend Barbara Gladney called from Albion. There was an excitement in her voice when she told me that she and I had been invited to Dallas. Albion, Michigan had been chosen an *All-America City* by the *National Civic League.* [13] I wasn't sure what it all meant.

She went on to say that it was a very prestigious award given to a community that works together to identify and tackle problems. The Melting Pot was acknowledged for its ability to relieve tension at a time when other communities were continuing to experience disastrous violence.

I couldn't travel to Dallas with Barbara; I had four little children and no one to take care of them. And at that point I was invested in focusing on only being a wife and mother. So Barbara flew to Texas and accepted the award on our behalf.

It's difficult to know why the Melting Pot did so well, but the lessons were life altering for Paul and me, and for many others. The story of Albion had begun with a simple meeting of minds and grew to feed us individually and as a community for many years. The city had been divided, but things changed. For whatever reason, people had agreed to trust each other and to let go. The good will, friendship, fabulous meals, and wonderful music had provided the foundation that had brought us to the higher ground of respecting and preserving a variety of cultures. Albion reflected our shared humanity and it had been everything that Wynton was not. In the face of what I knew had been unarguably a failure, I was comforted by recalling our success.

The fact that Albion had been chosen as an All-America City meant that our progress had been documented and real—the result of many people seeing the power in acceptance. The experience was fun—really fun—and fun unifies people.

It would be many years before we learned the truth about just how ugly it had gotten at the pub.

While I'd been taught to help others, my experiences with Frank and Julius taught me that I can't fix everything and that it

---

13 http://www.nationalcivicleague.org/aboutaac/

can be dangerous to try. At the very least we learned that Albion was as unique and wonderful as Wynton was disturbing.

At that point our family needed peace, so I bathed myself in gratitude for everything life had given me, and calmed my soul. I was blessed with the love of my children, and for the friends who stood by us through the worst of times; I felt a profound appreciation for my soul mate, and for the life we shared, my beautiful and now peaceful home, the beauty and warmth of a sunny day, the splash of raindrops on the windows, and for our good health.

Of course, change would come.

PART 4

CHAPTER TWENTY-NINE

The Medical Entertainments Begin

Not long after my rush of gratitude I found a worrisome lump just above Paul's left clavicle. As I rested my head on his chest while in our bed, the growth stood out like a rock. My heart sank.

Paul didn't think much about it. I told him he needed to go to the doctor—he said he was too busy. He was stubborn and resistant and told me to leave him alone—I didn't. I called the plant during the day, and when they said he was in a meeting, I asked them to pull him out.

With constant nagging, he buckled. One of life's great lessons for women—in cases like this, nagging works!

I immediately made an appointment with a surgeon, but after examination the doctor wasn't concerned. "It's a fatty tumor, a lipoma—we can take it or leave it," he said.

Paul said, "*Now*—will you stop?"

"*No, I won't!* It needs to come out."

"Well, it's clear you're not going to give this up. You win."

I rarely won arguments like this, but it was important enough for me to "go to the mat." As a nurse in the operating room I had examined many lumps and developed some skill in determining cancer—this lump scared me. I had never seen a lipoma in that area and doubted it was one.

Paul had the biopsy—a Hodgkin's Lymphoma. "There's no cure," the doctor announced, as we stood in the hall of the hospital surrounded by strangers. In 1973 there was no hope. The doctor continued. "Your husband could live up to five years, but it will more than likely be three."

I had done my best to prepare for the news, but it didn't help. I was sick inside. *How can I possibly live without him?*

As I internalized the prospect of my four children being fatherless, I felt totally alone in a town that had shown us little mercy. I knew I needed to do my homework.

We were fortunate to have an old friend in Boston who could help us make good decisions. I called Billy Southmayd, a skilled surgeon, one of Paul's roommates at Harvard—one of the "wild hooligans."

Our friends in Wynton had stuck by us through the Frank and Julius fiasco, and they did again for this. Charles, the plant manager, made arrangements for Paul to work in Massachusetts where he could be treated at great hospitals, and we'd have our families nearby to support us. What a hell of a way to finally get home.

Our friends had a spontaneous going-away party for us at the Wynton Country Club. Everyone arrived with good wishes and going-away gifts. Our departure was swift. On the day after the party, we packed up our children with a few belongings, and left for Boston. Judy and Cliff agreed to arrange for the sale of our house in our absence.

Billy had told us about an experimental NIH Grant program at the Peter Bent Brigham Hospital, and we wanted to get there as quickly as possible. Paul would have agreed to anything that gave him more than a zero chance to live.

During the week before heading east Paul had talked about having few regrets in life, and about wanting to teach his children how to sail before he "croaked." He was brave about his condition, and though he was always affectionate, he rarely showed the kind of tenderness I saw on this day.

We had no idea when we arrived in Boston that there was reason to hope. Thanks to Billy, Paul's doctor was William Maloney, a cutting-edge hematologist, who was identified as *the guy to get.* Dr. Maloney had experimented in the research lab he'd created in his home outside Boston.

Paul first had extensive testing for evaluation and mapping. Hodgkin's Disease generally follows a predictable track through the body. So the technicians mapped the course of the illness, the biopsies following surgery, and the cells of the tumor. He was in Stage 3.

Dr. Maloney said that Paul would be included in one of three treatment possibilities: chemotherapy, radiation, or a combination of both (more effective than the particularly caustic nitrogen mustard treatments of the early 1970s). The NIH would determine the effectiveness of the three approaches based on the outcomes and ultimately determine the best method of treatment. It was a crapshoot, but it made us hopeful. The odds of survival went up exponentially in Boston with any of these three options, but it would take five years to prove it.

Every patient involved in treatment had his or her spleen removed to stop the progression of the cancer. The lymph system is comprehensive, but nonetheless very predictable, and the tumor was contained in the lymph system.

After only one day Dr. Maloney decided it was time to take out Paul's spleen. "Time is of the essence," he had told us. "You have a chance of survival at this point, but your prognosis is contingent on the results of the surgical findings."

We drove to the hospital the night before the scheduled surgery. During the preparations Paul started vomiting violently. At one point, everything went dark and he nearly passed out. At first, they weren't sure what might have caused the near black out, but determined it might be anxiety because all his blood work had been negative for infection. The following day he had his spleen removed and tissue samples were sent to the lab to be analyzed. I waited at Paul's parents' house since they were as sick about this as I was. I held my breath as I waited for the surgeon's call.

When the doctor telephoned me after the operation, he didn't have great news—the lymph nodes in Paul's pelvis were enlarged, and the surgeon suspected that the cancer was already in Paul's belly.

Groggy and somber after surgery, he reached for my hand and said, "Please stay, I want to spend every possible minute with you, while I'm alive—every single minute."

I stayed with Paul for several hours, and when night came, the medication put him into a deep sleep. I went to my parents' house in Braintree. Two of the children were there and two were with my in-laws.

It was about a half-hour ride, and when I arrived I found my mother sitting with my Aunt Barbara at the kitchen table. I told them the doctor's news about the enlarged peritoneal lymph nodes and that the doctor *thought* the cancer was in Paul's abdomen.

My aunt and mother were at a loss, but tried to make me feel better. "It'll be OK, you'll see," my mother said.

Didn't they hear me? The doctor said the lymph nodes were enlarged. They must know how bad this is.

"No, Mom, it *won't* be OK."

They were trying to comfort me and I'd have none of it. It was unfair for me to treat them so badly. But, I couldn't make things easy for them at that moment, and they couldn't help me, either. So I got up and walked out, leaving my children with my mother. If they'd said, "Let's wait until the results of the biopsies come back before we come to conclusions," I could have heard it. Instead I wallowed in self-pity and in sympathy for my poor husband.

I was totally insensitive on that night. Both Paul's parents and mine were in terrible pain, too. Perhaps we could've found comfort in being together. But I just couldn't do it.

I got up from the table and ran out of the house. With the luxury of having my children cared for, I drove to the Goldbergs' house in Holbrook and parked my car in the same spot my old MG had been when it went off the cliff. I put my car in gear and pulled up the emergency break.

When I told my friends the results of the surgery, there was no denial. Jerry cried for a moment, and we all had two stiff drinks before I headed for their basement. Paul had renovated the space for them several years before, and somehow the memories of the good times we'd spent there gave me an element of comfort. I laid my head down on a full white pillow and fell into a deep sleep.

The following morning I awakened with a knot in the pit of my stomach. Reality struck. But the night of solid sleep allowed me to rally again.

Returning to Paul, I found him growling at the pain. Sometimes he was demanding, but I took all and any of Paul's responses in stride with the understanding that *he* was going through this, and I *wasn't*.

In the days that followed, a treatment plan was established for Paul that was based on the analysis of the tissue samples and the extent of the cancer's spread. When all the reports came back, I had trouble believing them. While they had found cancer cells in his neck and spleen, the enlarged pelvic nodes in his belly were benign. Paul had been fighting a *virus* on the night before his surgery when he passed out. He was in an early Stage 3 situation—we were hopeful again.

This report coupled with the new data on current treatment statistics changed Paul's original death sentence to a 50% chance of survival.

Paul and I sat looking at the doctor in shock. Neither of us let the feeling of joy penetrate for fear that we were hearing things differently, but when it hit us—what a gift!

When Paul and I got home we ate dinner and together we put the kids to bed early. We had stopped to buy a bottle of expensive wine on the way home, and when the kids were sleeping soundly, we drank it. I kissed his face, and his arms, and the nape of his neck. I kissed him everywhere, and hugged him, and we both relished the prospect of a long life together.

We struggled to keep some balance in our children's lives and decided not to share the extent of Paul's illness with them. We wanted our children to feel secure in the midst of it all, and it wasn't hard, because there was love all around them. After having been separated from them geographically since they were born, their grandparents were happy to have them around.

While I didn't think about what our parents had done for us in the beginning, I came to appreciate them immensely in the years that followed. Fred had decided that I had saved his son's life, and his attitude toward me changed. I also had a greater appreciation of his finer characteristics of loyalty and dedication to his family.

Through all of Paul's "medical entertainment," we thought little about Frank and Julius. The trauma of our current situation had trimmed the sharp edges off our experiences in Wynton. After we'd learned of Paul's illness and moved to Massachusetts, the memories of Frank and Julius remained locked in the past. It became convenient, and mandatory, to leave it all behind and live in the moment; anything but 'now' was irrelevant.

CHAPTER THIRTY

Back To New England

When Paul's treatment began in the spring of 1973, we lived with his parents and sometimes with mine. Each day our oldest daughter Lisa walked from my parents' house to my old elementary school where she was in the first grade. One of my former elementary school teachers had become a principal, and took Lisa under her wing for the remainder of the year. Later in the year we bought a house near Boston, in Medfield. There were no factories in Massachusetts, so the company generously allowed Paul to work in sales and that allowed us stay in the Boston area.

Once Paul started full body radiation, there was only a small window of time where he could eat without being sick, but he managed to become the only person known to gain weight on radiation at Peter Bent Brigham Hospital. Paul was determined to give it his best, and approached his illness like he does everything else. He studied his body rhythms and knew when he was likely to get sick. He had it down to a science.

When it was time for us to move into our new house, Paul was still in the throes of radiation therapy. As the lawyers scurried around the bank at the house closing, he got fed up with the massive amounts of paperwork, and their chaos.

"Look, you guys, why aren't you ready? I just had a radiation treatment this morning and only have about five minutes before I start throwing up all over the table. Can we *please* get on with it?"

It was terrific to be back in New England; my parents came to visit often and we visited them in Braintree as well. My father relished having the children home, and when we needed it, loving child-care was available.

During our initial experience in Medfield I was focused on helping Paul through his treatments while making sure that our children got a decent education; we were told that the town had superior schools.

We lived in Medfield through his treatment and surgical recovery without noticing the nature of the community. By the time the radiation treatment ended, we realized that the demographic was different than it had been in Wynton—though everyone was white here as well, they were highly educated and had high incomes.

Subsequent to the radiation treatment, Paul's chances of survival increased month by month, hitting 80% six months after surgery. We had escaped again.

Paul rarely had to work at being happy—it was his nature. He had approached his illness with the attitude that he would use every minute of every day happily. I always envied him.

He simply decided not to worry about his remission. His entire body had been radiated, and it was inconceivable that even one migrant cell could have survived. He had shown extraordinary courage, and humor became his best friend. Stepping completely out of character became comedic to him, and he took pleasure in outrageous behaviors that went far beyond the bounds of decency.

Some of my Italian aunts had been certain that Paul would die, and in traditional Pasquale drama, their every action reflected a "poor Paul" mantra that was intolerable to him.

When his hair fell out, my cousin Dolores painted a woman's face on the back of his bald head. This was the least unusual of his bizarre coping mechanisms.

Once he told my aunts that he wished to be waked in the nude, and they responded in horror. He then followed up with "OK, how about this here suit I'm wearing, would this be OK to wear at the wake?"

"No, no, don't say that," Aunt Cookie pleaded.

I thought he was very mean, and told him he'd gone too far, but he looked at me with a boyish grin, ignored my comment, and went on to enjoy his sick banter when the opportunity arose.

CHAPTER THIRTY-ONE

Paul-Otics

My husband Paul and his friend Paul Guzzi had been very close in college, and "Guzzi" had been an usher at our wedding. He was, in fact, another of the "hooligan college roommates" my old boyfriend Bob had deemed sinners. Paul Guzzi was dear. It was he who had given my husband the nick name *Pudge* after his belly grew fat from eating too much at *the Grill* where Julia Child had yelled at him for infesting her kitchen with germs.

To help Paul Guzzi get elected to the office of *Secretary of State,* we had set up campaign activities in our living room. He'd been a State Representative for several years, but becoming *Secretary of State* was a long shot because the incumbent had held the office for years, and they were both Democrats. Nonetheless, Paul Guzzi won the election.

Within a week after the election, he and his wife Joanne came over to our house with their children. The newly elected Secretary of State brought a bottle of Scotch; and the two Pauls sat on our back porch and drank enough to get honest. The kids played as Joanne and I watched the two men exchanging words.

"I can't believe I won!" Guzzi said. "You've got to come, Pudge. I need to hire honest people who know what they're doing. You're the only one I can think of who's ever managed anything."

"I have a job Guzz! Why would I come and work for the likes of you?"

"Because you *should*, and it'll be a good time," Guzzi said.

"OK, my friend, I'll try to get a leave of absence from my job for a year or two, but we can't hire political hacks, and the no-shows must go," my husband said.

"Why do you think I ran in the first place? Of course we'll do whatever we need to do to get rid of the hacks and make things better."

When Paul Pimentel woke up on the following morning with a headache, he asked, "Holy shit! What did I agree to last night?"

"You agreed to leave your job for a year or two to help your friend in his new job, that's what you did," I said.

On the day of my husband's induction to his new job as Deputy Secretary of State, I sat with the kids in the front row of the State House Chamber, as they watched their father promise the governor that he would do everything but stand up and sing "The Star-Spangled Banner" in Fenway Park.

At the reception in the rotunda after the ceremony, the kids ran around statues of various patriots that were scattered throughout the magnificent room. When it was over, we walked up to his new office. It was large and full of history. There was a beautiful wooden fireplace and the Colonial ambience made me wonder just how many important decisions had been made there since Charles Bulfinch designed it in 1798. *This is great*, I thought.

Susan, Sandy, Lisa, Paul, Joanie and Chris

One of the first things that my Paul did when he took his new job was to deal with the *no-show* son of a prominent legislator (who was serving as budget committee vice chairman), and it proved to be problematic.

Paul had asked the legislator how to handle the situation and reported to Guzzi the results of his conversation. "Do whatever you have to do with my son," the legislator had said with vigor. Neither Paul Guzzi nor the employee's father thought that meant firing the man. But after several chances, Paul P. let him go and said he was incorrigible. Attempting to carry out the firing with sensitivity didn't matter.

When Paul P. saw their budget devastated in response to the firing, he realized he'd been naive. He told the budget-cutting legislator, "The Secretary of State's office will be paralyzed—there'll be no elections without a reasonable budget. You simply can't do this!"

The legislator said, "Oh yeah, watch me."

Both Pauls were stunned, and Paul P. was relegated to begging the House for funding with a seasoned political ally, Jack McGlynn, who accompanied him to the committee chair's office. With an impish smirk on his face, Jack said about my husband Paul, "The kid means well." This was not the only firing that created problems.

Another hack had been fired without *his* benefactor being notified. This too created huge budget problems. But Guzzi saved the day on this one by playing squash with the offended politician. Paul Guzzi was a much more skilled politician than his friend and roommate. In the end it was all good, and the hacks never returned.

It didn't take long for the little old ladies in the office to feel good about what was going on. They'd been working diligently for decades while the hacks and no-shows skated along doing nothing. The two Pauls were popular, and the remaining staff and new hires were happy to work hard.

While Paul went into the state house every day, I dragged Joanie to various meetings. She was only in nursery school for half days when I took to standing on street corners in support of the Equal Rights Amendment; after Paul's illness I came to see how important it was for women to be paid equally, and to be treated with equal respect and dignity. The risk of losing my husband had inspired a growing awareness of the economic reality of the single mother.

One drizzly day when the kids were in school, I put Joanie in the stroller and headed for the corner in front of the school with my sign. It was Election Day and the amendment was on the ballet. I had told the local League of Women Voters that I would stand there for the day.

As the rain began to fall, the dampness penetrated my coat. I made sure Joanie was bundled and protected as I held the sign over my head. As people passed by, I'd smile and give them the thumbs up.

She was almost three, and getting old for the stroller, but I was able to keep her occupied with songs and riddles between hellos and goodbyes until it was time to drop her off at nursery school.

When I got back to the corner, the gentle rain had become torrential. I held my soggy sign up and stood there for two more hours with my clothes stuck to my breasts like a second skin, and my hair dripping water down my back.

Then I picked up Joanie at nursery school and ran home in time to meet the kids after school. They were to play at two different neighbors' houses for the following two hours. I packed the four of them up, dropped them off, and headed back to hold my sign on the street corner in the pelting rain.

At the end of the day, I put the drooping *EQUAL RIGHTS FOR WOMEN* sign in the car. I picked up the children and went home to make dinner in time for Paul's arrival from work.

How is it possible that I didn't see the irony of this day?

The equal rights amendment passed in Massachusetts.

Now that we were home in Massachusetts, I was excited that we could have parties at our house. My cousin Dolores planned a family hayride in the town next to us. I was convinced that having a horse drag us across an open field on a pile of hay lacked imagination. So I invited my parents, aunts, uncles, and cousins to come back to our house when it was over.

The sun was just setting when we arrived at the barn to start the hayride. My relatives were always game for fun, but unlikely participants of such an event—my aunts with their perfectly groomed jet-black coiffures, carefully arched eyebrows, and high-heeled shoes.

My father and his brothers sat neatly on the back of the wagon looking dapper; these were the days of polyester. My cousin Dolores and I would joke about how they never could pass by a mirror without at least a quick glance. Paul accused me of being worthy of the reputation.

As the wagon moved through the subtle but distinct aroma of early fall, a large orange moon slowly rose up, and then seemed to almost stop in the deep blue of evening. As they all began singing softly in perfect harmony, I felt like I was in a movie.

When the hayride was over, Paul and I were the first ones to leave the field. I wanted to prepare the final touches for the party. When we arrived home I dismissed the babysitter who had tucked all of our kids into bed safely and soundly. Then I set out a buffet.

The others soon followed and some meandered onto our screened porch, while a few chose to sit around our swimming pool. As a result of the unusually hot summer, it was still pleasant out and the pool remained warmer than the air.

In the wake of his life-threatening episode, Paul continued with his antics. While people were eating, he slipped quietly into the water and took off his bathing suit. At first no one noticed as his butt dipped and splashed in and out of the water like a frolicking dolphin, but eventually my Aunt Terry shrieked—and all eyes turned to his unforgiving bare buttocks. Paul is a good-looking man, but his baggy ass is not his most attractive feature. Even he was aghast when he saw it reflected in a mirror.

The initial shock inspired squeals which turned to chuckles and then to belly laughs.

I couldn't believe Paul had chosen *my* family as audience for this exhibition, but I realized his antics were helping him through the toughest of times. Having just completed entire body radiation, he knew he could get away with just about anything. I decided it was easier to join than fight him, so I added some spice of my own to the scenario—no, I didn't go naked.

After Paul had wrapped a towel around himself strategically to cover the *boys,* he entered the screened porch and went to get clothes. I was thankful that at least he had the decency to do that.

When he emerged from the bedroom, I was ready. I had retrieved a huge banana cream pie from the refrigerator (I had several), and as he approached the porch, I strategically swung it at him with notable force. The whipped cream and bananas struck his face with a smashing blow.

Once my hit had registered, I ran out the porch door, as Paul chased me with the remains of the pie. In the end we were both covered in whipped cream and bananas, laughing hysterically, and then laughing some more.

My aunts were thrilled with the entertainment. It was rare for them to be upstaged at a party, and even my father sat back at this one.

On the night of the hayride in 1973, my cousin, Robert Angelo (Bobby), had brought his new girlfriend Joanne, a pretty young Italian woman, to the party to introduce her to the family. By that time he was a state representative and he expected the usual dancing and singing, joke telling, and folklore. In spite of the bizarre turn of events, they ultimately married, and it became a night they never forgot.

After we'd lived in Medfield for a couple of years, I fell into a significant and anxiety-ridden depression. I'd always been strong in the face of disaster, but the trauma of Vietnam, Paul's illness, and the episode in Wynton had taken its toll. While I had the capacity to enjoy any given moment exuberantly, I would often suffer in silence in the hours between.

While Paul lived in the moment all the time, I continued to fight for happiness. Perhaps I was wired like my aunts on both sides—they too were anxious and miserable between episodes of elation.

But living in Medfield with four kids and little gratification in the aftermath of trauma was more than I could handle. I began seeing a psychiatrist who reminded me of Peter Sellers in "The Pink Panther" scene where his nose was melting as he tried to pull the inspector's teeth out. The scene took place in a castle just before the world was supposed to come to an end.

I came to refer to the psychiatrist as "Peter." He was distant and seemed almost ineffectual, but in my weakened state, I assumed he knew more about *me* than I did. Once he actually fell asleep while I was telling him about my feelings of impending doom.

There were days in Medfield when my depression was particularly crippling—sometimes I was so anxious I thought I was dying and other times I wasn't sure I had the desire to live. But I had to. I was never really the kind of person who could consider ending my life, and at that time I still had the worry of children and a medically-challenged husband. My life had become a trap and my only option was to try to exist without drowning.

Things got worse. I started calling Paul too often at work, and imagined that I had cancer. I was short with the kids, and when they were in school, I went back to bed and stayed there until they got home.

"Peter" said I had a panic disorder. Every morning when I opened my eyes, I felt like I was about to be struck by an oncoming train. I was helpless. I knew things weren't right, but I felt there was little I could do about it.

At first "Peter" prescribed a tranquilizer. The anxiety diminished, but the depression escalated. When I realized that I'd become addicted to the tranquilizer, I stopped taking it. It was hard to do and when it was over I felt worse than when I'd begun.

It was then that my *make-shift* psychiatrist put me on an antidepressant. The medication took the edge off both the anxiety and the depression, but I had no idea what I was feeling or why, and neither did *he*.

Paul had difficulty relating to what was happening. While he had experienced pain and sadness, his emotions always had been connected to something he could understand cognitively.

For the first time my emotional state consumed me. But as time went on, I tried to find meaningful activities for my life in Medfield.

The time was approaching when Paul would return to his job. He considered two options. He *could* stay comfortably in the State House. But he was an engineer at heart and to be away from any sort of technical challenge was to negate a vital part of himself. Paul had enjoyed the experience and challenge of working in government, but it was not his first choice.

He and his friend Paul Guzzi had done well together. With shared values, they were both principled, stubborn, and neither was afraid of risk; they had different but compatible skill sets. Paul Guzzi frequently referred to my husband as a stabilizing force, and they genuinely liked and respected each other. Together they were able to organize and manage the state census, and to finish it *on* time. This had never happened.

In addition the office had stayed within the budget for the first time in history. They were able to run elections, start a *State House Book Store*—for ordering government, historical, and legal documents, and construct and open a *Citizens Information Service*. When they were able to eliminate the necessity of taking a state census by submitting a constitutional amendment allowing the state to utilize the federal census indefinitely, millions of Bay State tax payer dollars were saved.

In the end Paul Guzzi happily had kept his promise to Paul about the "hacks and no shows." They had run into political hurdles because of it, but Paul G. was always able to take the heat and resolve any resulting crisis. The learning experience had been invaluable for both of them. When the work was done, the office got too small for two big men.

In the years following my husband's experience in state government, he always would be proud to have served with his smart, hard-working, and scrupulously honest friend. But for now, it was time to move on.

Shortly after Paul decided to leave the Office of the Secretary of State, he made an announcement that would thrust the trajectory of our future into uncertainty. "I want to start my own energy conservation consulting company, and I want to build a solar house as a prototype."

Without a thought, I said, "OK." That's the way it was back then. Women just went with the flow without question. Trusting Paul was easy; he generally was able to do whatever he set his mind to.

During the year I'd been on medication, the depression and anxiety had diminished. But it hadn't been without sacrifice. While I'd been more able to cope with the tedium—and with the aftermath of trauma—my emotions came only in the shade of beige. I longed for the passion of red, orange, and yellow. Years would pass before I could call myself a truly happy person.

CHAPTER THIRTY-TWO

Moving On – Again

We decided to leave Medfield. So we explored a little to see where things might be better. Boston was suffering in the aftermath of desegregation (busing); the social justice issues were more widespread than we'd realized.

We discovered the demographics in Hingham were pretty much the same as Medfield. But, while the town lacked diversity, it was willing to show some semblance of social responsibility by allowing inner city kids to join ours. METCO[14] (a program that bused inner city school kids to the suburbs) was likely to be passed

14 "The Metco Program is a grant program funded by the Commonwealth of Massachusetts. It is a voluntary program intended to expand educational opportunities, increase diversity, and reduce racial isolation, by permitting students in certain cities to attend public schools in other communities that have agreed to participate.

"The Program has been in existence since 1966 and was originally funded through a grant by the Carnegie Foundation and United States Office of Education. In that year the first Metco legislation was filed, METCO Inc. was established, and seven school districts began accepting the first two hundred Metco students. Currently, there are about 3,300 students participating in 33 school districts in metropolitan Boston and at four school districts outside Springfield."
http://www.doe.mass.edu/metco/

in the near future, and that gave us some confidence about the town.

The beauty of Hingham coupled with the excellent school system settled it for us.

We arrived in Hingham with little money. We had the opportunity to buy a house on the ocean for a fabulous price on Causeway Road, but decided to rent it instead so that Paul could build his solar experiment to help his new business. I went along with renting instead of buying the house like a goddamned fool! Paul didn't entertain failure in business as an option, and he started his new company on a shoestring.

When Paul had been sick, he'd talked about not having had the chance to teach the children to sail. Now we had a house on the water. He bought a little sailboat for $800. And so we had a little less.

The rental house we lived in while waiting to build the solar house was situated on a coastal lot protected from the open ocean—on a tiny street that served as a miniature peninsula. It was a peaceful house with trees around it and water on both sides. We moved in the spring, and the kids started school shortly thereafter. It didn't take me long to settle in. The north side of the house was glass, and across the sloped lawn was a private beach with a slip for Paul's new boat. Our parents were happy; we lived just twenty minutes away.

What a place—in the summer with the windows open, the sea breeze found its way to our bedroom. At night in bed we could hear the waves hit the beach in gentle succession, a romantic aphrodisiac.

Sometimes as I sat in my yard watching the white sails of small boats passing by, the scent of salt air would magnify the experience of the sea. Women often sunned themselves in the heat of the day while their young children splashed in the calm shallows. In those moments I felt lucky—and then guilty.

In spite of all my good fortune, I was anxious—I wasn't worried about me dying any more, but rather about my kids drowning in the ocean in my own back yard. The anxiety was ever-present. I was thinking irrationally, and I knew it.

My depression didn't need to be related to anything but my own chemistry, and it was sometimes connected to events that hung in the back of the mind like an old shirt forgotten in the back of the closet.

It was so much easier when I was clueless, I thought.

When I was eighteen I supported Richard Nixon—right and wrong were *clearly* defined *for* me. By my mid-thirties I'd learned about trickle-down poverty and how it relates to racism, and how racism relates to oppression, and how oppression relates to crime and violence. And I had experienced it first-hand in Wynton.

As I sat quietly under a tree overlooking the ocean, I wondered about Frank and Julius. It'd been four years since that horrible night. "Julius had come so close to seizing an opportunity." I thought I might never know what had really happened.

My life of contemplation was brief. After almost a decade of being a stay-at-home mom, I went back to work on the evening shift in the operating room at the local hospital—and I was terrified. All the surgeries would be done in crisis; in the first week there were two emergency ruptured aortic aneurisms. I was thankful that Joe Iovino was the surgeon on duty that week; surgeons could often be testy, but Joe kept everything calm and professional in the throes of life and death.

Joanie was in Kindergarten, Susan was in first grade, Chris was in second, and Lisa was in fourth.

My salary was not nearly enough to support our family, but my godfather, Don Remick, had passed away and left me enough money for us to survive on until Paul got his company off the ground.

Arriving home from the hospital at night anxious and exhausted, I couldn't sleep for the first month. In my absence, Paul was left at home to make tuna surprise for the kids. He thought he could be a stay-at-home Dad and build his business at the same time; he quickly learned that his new job was difficult.

He'd take a can of cream of mushroom soup, mix it with a can of tuna and some baby peas, and bake it with some biscuits on top. At first he was a star, but the novelty soon wore off, and in a short time the kids were miserable. So I made dinners and froze them.

When our kids came home from school, I was about to leave, and when I came home at night, they were asleep. Come the weekend, sometimes I would be working and other times we would be tied up with various family challenges; once all four kids caught lice at school and it took us a full weekend to get rid of them. The weekends were just insane.

CHAPTER THIRTY-THREE

The Blizzard of '78[15]

A blizzard was predicted to hit in the late afternoon of February 6th. By that time I was working the 7 AM to 3 PM shift at the hospital. I had a treacherous ride home. When I arrived, Paul was in the living room with three of the kids.

"Where's Susan?" I asked in a panic.

"She's playing at her friend's, she'll be home soon," Paul said.

"Are you aware there's a blizzard going on and that I *barely* made it home? Look out the window!"

He looked up and acted like he always did when he thought I was *over*-reacting. I called the neighbor, and the father answered. "Oh—she just left a few minutes ago."

I was too worried to be angry; I grabbed my coat and rushed out to find my seven-year old daughter. The wind cut across the top of the hill with determination, and a white sheet of snow already covered the back yard where the steep, rocky hill slanted down to the small inlet.

I could barely see Susan in the distance. She was struggling to walk up the hill through the gusts. I fought the wind and snow, but before I could get to her, she fell to the ground and began to slide across the icy yard. I chased her, afraid that she would keep

15 The tragic storm followed on the heels of another that dropped 21 inches on January 21st. View a collection of photos from CBS NEWS of the record 27.1 inches of snow in the Boston area. http://www.cbsnews.com/pictures/the-blizzard-of-1978/

blowing away from me, and then over the rocky descent—short work for the northeast wind to move a small child.

She extended her arm, and I grabbed it, the wind lifting her whole body into the air. I pulled her toward me and held her tightly as we approached the house. When I flung open the door, the wind propelled us into the room as the door banged hard against the wall of the living room.

Paul said "*Hello,*" as if he was greeting a group of ladies at an afternoon tea. He'd been reading some engineering plans while the kids were playing. Not one of them seemed to have noticed the icy wind coming off the ocean and slamming against the plate glass windows in the living room or the sideways slant of the snow that negated the view beyond an inch of the window.

How can I leave my children with such a man? I asked myself. I didn't talk to him until we got into bed that night.

"What are you so mad about?" he asked.

"The fact that you need to ask is one of the biggest reasons. You allowed a child to fight a blizzard all alone, for God's sake."

"She would have been fine. The neighbors thought so, too, and that's why they sent her home."

I thought, *The neighbors must have neglected to look out the window and you must have had your nose buried in the dark place.*

At that moment I thought about leaving my job.

Paul's coach in high school was right, I thought. *He is, in fact, an idiot with a high IQ.*

The next morning the sun showed bright and beautiful on an exquisite landscape—frosted trees and a white, glistening yard unmarred by a single footprint. The wind had shaved the snow down to a frosted icy glare and drifted in some places higher than Paul's chest.

We all bundled up and found our way down to a mound of snow that stood almost even with Paul's eyes, and together we started to build an igloo. Paul, the all-knowing engineer was the supervisor. The rest of us carried out orders until the magnificent sculptured icehouse was completed.

Our neighbors had lost power, but we were spared. Our neighborhood had not been plowed, something none of us had ever experienced.

Since we had heat and the use of a stove, we invited the neighbors over with their kids for an impromptu party. They all brought food, wine, and half-full bottles of alcohol; some drank more than they should have. Looking out on the winter wonderland inspired a feeling of awe.

The following day, a truck pulled up to take me to work at the hospital. Large and able to drive through almost anything, it was open in the back, like my grandfather's. I hopped in to join several doctors and nurses who had been picked up before me, and sat next to Joe Iovino.

As we drove to pick up others in the freezing breeze, our faces began to stiffen in the chill, and as we chatted, my mouth could barely move. I learned that Joe lived across the street from the site of our new house.

We chatted for the entire hour it took to arrive at the hospital. Our faces were red from the wind and we could barely blink.

CHAPTER THIRTY-FOUR

Midlife Crisis

As time went on, our marriage changed. While at work, I missed my kids. When Paul was with them, his mind was usually on some engineering project. Our daughter, Joanie, would stay awake at night and wait until I got home—she missed me. Neither Paul nor the kids were happy with the situation, but we were determined to make the best of it.

It didn't take long to realize that Paul doesn't do well as a subordinate. His life had changed enormously. One day he was solving intricate engineering problems and had 250 employees responding to his beck and call, and the next, he was at the beck and call of four children, and dealing with mundane daily problems like a missing sock in the dryer.

In response to our new dynamic, he began to withdraw and withhold. He was no longer making an income and he was struggling every day to build a business that didn't have a market; nobody cared about saving energy in 1978, and, in essence, Paul felt emasculated. A man in a woman's role in those days was considered a free-loader.

I felt alone, but my depression had diminished; work was empowering. I continued, however, to experience intractable anxiety. I missed the closeness of our superb relationship. For the first time in our marriage, Paul was pulling away from me, and I didn't know how to change that. It appeared to be a midlife crisis of enormous proportions.

When he could no longer tolerate the situation, he made a shocking pronouncement—"There's nobody else or anything like that, but I just want to leave, I need to flee."

I was completely caught off guard—but in some ways—relieved. The emotional stalemate had ended and he had drawn a line in the sand; anything was better than living in a limbo of resentment.

I sat wounded for a minute, but my instincts saved me. *I am a strong woman*, I told myself, *a very strong woman*. I looked directly at Paul and quietly and confidently said, "If you think that's what you want, you should go. I can't make this right for you."

Paul and I had grown up in the middle of a cultural revolution. He had become a *stay at home dad* when it was thought to be beneath a man's dignity. When he would take Joanie to the bus stop, and stand with the group of mothers, he felt like a *dupe*. I think he was embarrassed that I was working while he stayed home.

Raising kids isn't easy work, and feeling unappreciated is difficult, especially when you've had people responding to your every request. *Welcome to my world*, I had said to myself. I had felt the same way when Paul was in Southeast Asia for months at a time, or on lonely nights when he was in remote parts of the country. But I believed that if I waited long enough, the love would emerge from the chaos of emotions and come alive again.

I didn't want to sleep with Paul that night, but I decided that if he wanted to leave, the bed was mine. *He* chose to sleep next to me, though, and I found this curious.

Silently, in the dead of night, I stared at the ceiling wondering what Paul was thinking. I knew he was doing the same.

By morning he realized his emotional confusion could cost him life as he knew it. *"What the hell am I doing?"* he had asked himself—and then me. "I have everything!"

"Yes, you do," I said. And softly, I repeated, "Yes, you do."

While Paul was confused, he wasn't stupid, so he pulled himself together and had the sense to let the dust settle.

I gave him the time he needed to do it.

I knew our new life had robbed him of his identity, and that he felt failure, without ever having failed. He was depressed for the first time since we'd been together—perhaps for the first time in his life. I was sympathetic.

Eventually he figured it all out. When his business started to take shape, he could see more clearly, and in time, he could openly talk about what he was feeling. He even began to value the year he'd spent with his children, and realized that he was closer to them because of the experience.

"I think I was very sad," he finally announced. "When I said out loud that I wanted to leave, you reacted in a way that kept me from getting caught in the struggle. When it hit me that I'd said I wanted to leave *you*, I felt even more powerless. It was the situation I wanted to leave—you must have known I never could've done it."

"God only knows what you would have done if you had to change smelly diapers," I teased.

Paul and I got completely back on track.

CHAPTER THIRTY-FIVE

Solar Panels and Sitting Bull

When the ground thawed in the spring, we were able to dig the foundation for our new house. We were in for a family learning adventure, but the kids weren't excited about leaving their friends or the ocean—and neither was I.

When the process began, Paul was the designer and taskmaster. I was the great and general contractor—responsible for finding subcontractors, and calling the (usually drunk) carpenters when they didn't show up to work. The children had specific duties as well; Paul taught them how to do all sorts of things like masonry, dipping barn board into stain, and landscaping.

Once the basic structure was built, it looked like a colonial farmhouse. The house was super insulated and had some innovative features that made the neighbors in our upscale Hingham neighborhood think we were a bit *off the mark*. Large windows lined the first and second floor of the entire south side. Paul wanted to save every possible BTU, so he installed windows that were smaller than most on the north, east, and west sides. It all looked rather incomplete. But, when we put white shutters on the windows, they came alive. They looked nice against the grey barn-board.

Paul ordered quilted, white shades for the large windows in the back of the house to keep the heat *in* when the sun wasn't *out*, and it took a long time for them to be cut to size and finished.

We'd bought a one-piece fiberglass pool. Foam insulation had been sprayed on the bottom to help retain heat for the house during the winter months. Two Italian brothers dug the foundation, landscaped the property, and prepared the ground for the installation of the pool.

The Iaria brothers were lively characters and somehow I felt like we were related. They worked hard every day, and at noon they'd pull out a basket with cheese, bread, and Italian cold cuts for lunch.

Paul loved these guys, and when he could, he'd sit under the only tree in the yard with them and listen to their hilarious stories while they ate their lunch. At the end of the day we'd sometimes invite them to stay for a glass of Chianti.

On the day that the pool was set in the ground, the brothers left expecting to return the following day to fill the soil around it.

My children and I sat in our living room looking through the expanse of the south-facing windows. Dark black clouds roiled in the distance and the sun disappeared. A bolt of lightning came zigzagging to earth and for a second it felt like it was in the room; a crash of thunder shook the house almost simultaneously.

As the sky opened up, torrential rain began to flow into the bottom of the opening around the massive fiberglass structure. As the water accumulated around the foam insulation on the bottom of the pool, I noticed a hint of movement. I moved away from the windows, anticipating the inevitable.

The pool suddenly blooped upward and started bobbing like a huge ark only a few feet away from the wall of windows. As it tipped up and down and back and forth, I could only hope that it remained on the other side of the living room wall. We were all amazed. When the last drop of rain had fallen, I called Paul in his new office in Boston.

"Honey, you'd better come home with two elephants, two giraffes, and a variety of other animals, I think God is dropping a hint." The pool was sitting diagonally across the yard, and I had no idea how it would be set back into the hole where it had once been housed.

On the first Christmas in our new solar (off the grid) house, there was little sun. We all wore hats and could see our breath as we sat around the living room opening gifts. The entire floor of the living room was covered with torn wrapping paper. The kids started mocking their father's experiment, and the fact that their only consolation was in taking the very short Navy showers that Paul had given them license to take.

I realized *then* we were living in an experimental solar lab—pioneering in the twentieth century. Before we'd moved to Berkley Circle, Paul talked about building a house *into* the side of a hill. At that moment, I was grateful he hadn't been able to find an appropriate lot for such a house. I didn't fancy living in a cave.

After the pool had been safely installed, next came the ceramic floor designed to hold heat. Unusual and expensive—I'd chosen it because it was pretty. Paul had wanted black to hold the heat, but I told him I wasn't going to live in a dungeon when the sun wasn't out. On gloomy days, the shades needed to be down to hold the heat.

On a frigid January day in 1979, the sunlight poured into the house and the heat began to accumulate shortly after dawn. Sweat dripped from the brows of the workers as they laid the tiles. Here it was the dead of winter with an interior temperature soaring into the nineties, and the smell of B.O. permeating the living room.

"Can you turn the heat down?" one workman asked.

"The heat isn't on—we have no heat," I explained.

"How can there be no heat on, it's ten outside?"

"Good question. Ask my husband about that."

If I'd put the shades down we wouldn't have been able to collect enough heat to keep us warm that night, so I offered the poor men pitchers of ice water, and wished them my best.

Paul wanted to formally collect data, so he worked with our friend Steven Rudnick, an MIT engineer, to develop a computer model to manage the heat in the house and the swimming pool and to open and close the insulated shades.

Computers were a relatively new concept for the average person, and they were big. Paul and Steven had a grand old time talking about BTUs, heat loss, and the like. Unbeknownst to me, Paul cut a gaping hole in our living room wall to accommodate his exciting new computer.

I was furious. "How could you put an ugly thing like this in such a prominent place?" I asked. "And why didn't you ask me where it should go?"

"I didn't think it was a big deal," Paul answered.

"Well, it goddamn is. There's a huge fucking hole in the middle of the wall of our living room. (We'd gotten over the "no swearing in front of me" practice, and I'd started using the "F" word occasionally because I found it empowering.)

"I know you and Steve will be pondering that computer for the next *century*, and in the meantime, I'll be staring at an *enormous* black hole," I said indignantly.

"OK, I'll fill it in and change the location to the den closet," Paul said.

"And when might *that* be?"

"When I get a chance . . ."

I didn't wait for Paul to solve the problem. Paul Guzzi had gifted Paul a large lithograph of Sitting Bull when he left the State House, and I hung it over the hole until I could find something more fitting.

Our solar house was completed in 1978.

CHAPTER THIRTY-SIX

My Turn

Lois Rudnick was an amazing teacher, a scholar, a good friend, and married to Steven, our computer guy, genius friend. When she spoke, I listened. She was writing a book about Mabel Dodge Luhan whose claim to fame was that she kept company with the likes of D.H. Lawrence, Emma Goldman, Georgia O'Keefe, Willa Cather—just to name a few. Mabel was a magnet for various art communities, and she sparked an interest in the arts through a variety of networks.

Mabel was perfect for Lois, and Lois was perfect for me. She was the person I needed to get me moving intellectually; she was yet another friend in the relentless pursuit of my best interests.

Lois had deemed herself to be Queen of the Universe, and I became one of her maids in waiting. In 1982, Lois started harassing me to go back to school—specifically the University of Massachusetts in Boston where she was a professor.

"You're too damn smart to stay away from college," Lois insisted. "You *must* go back to school!" My excuse that I had four young children to raise was greeted with, "Just apply."

So, I did.

I left my job in the hospital and took a position as a nurse in a day treatment program for chronically mentally ill clients. I got accepted to UMASS Boston and went back to college at the same time. I transferred some of my nursing credits, and persevered.

My office was only fifteen minutes away, so I was able to get home in time to make dinner and be with the kids on most nights.

The kids were involved in various activities like gymnastics, Pop Warner football, Little League, music lessons—it went on and on. I consolidated my classes to one night a week and Saturday mornings. Somehow it all worked—or didn't. I did the best I could.

In May 1984 I received a BA in Management of Human Services from *UMASS Boston*. My children all sat together with my husband and friends at my graduation, and I felt a profound sense of accomplishment. After the ceremony, we had a party at our solar house in the middle of the cornfield on Berkley Circle.

To legitimize Lois's *Queen of the Universe* status, I presented her with a brass crown with *not so real* emeralds and rubies. Lois—who told me that with my new degree I could now serve at her right hand—had made a profound difference in my life.

My hope was that as a registered nurse with a management degree, I would be more marketable. But before I graduated, I was offered a job in the District Attorney's Office as Director of Human Services. This was a title that I had no business owning, but the DA, Bill Delahunt, was sure I was the person for the job. He was known to be a master at recruiting staff. I had worked on his campaign when he left the House of Representatives to run for District Attorney, and he and his wife Kati were old friends. He had asked me to help him find someone to fill the position of Director of Human Services in his office.

I had set up some interviews for him when he told me he wanted me to take the job. I told him I didn't think I was a good choice, but he insisted. After much deliberation I quit my job at the Department of Mental Health and went to work for Bill.

The job went to my head at first, and I didn't listen enough to people around me. It took me years to become good at what I was doing, because emotionally I wasn't ready to take on such responsibility. I took risks and was lucky that good came from many of them in spite of my inexperience and boundary issues. Somehow Bill Delahunt saw through it all and allowed me the time to grow.

Chapter Thirty-Seven

Our Children

When our children were growing up they often took dangerous risks, and at times I felt like a really bad mother. But in the end, the goodness and competence of our children prevailed in spite of us.

The kids were free spirited and creative as teens and they had my affinity for music. Our house was always full of instruments, and the voices and noise of young people jamming. Even those who couldn't sing or play an instrument became joyful in the face of the music at our house, and as time went on, the parades resumed with used, real, and makeshift instruments.

Not only were our children creative—they were also effective in their efforts to save others. They had the same propensity for random acts of kindness as my father. Reminiscent of the night my father brought home the freezing man and stuck him in bed with his brothers, it seemed our children were programmed genetically to bring young people home, often believing I could *fix* them. Our house became a magnet for kids who felt unsafe and unloved.

Because of this many kids came through our doors on Berkley Circle. Most were sent our way after we became an emergency placement home for the *Department of Social Services*. Many of these children were in crisis and deemed runners, but they never ran—not from us, anyway. Some were friends of our own children; others were placed with us officially.

Concerned about their friend Courtney, our daughters brought her home and asked if I'd speak to her. She'd been born in Korea and brought up in America by a Caucasian family who were ill-equipped to care for her.

It was a crazy time as our house was filled with kids, Courtney being one of them. Fewer teens and more structure would have been more reasonable. Our children paid the price. It was a miracle they emerged sophisticated and happy participants in life.

By the time Courtney was sixteen, we had been granted custody and became her parents. In late October of 1987, we rented a hall, invited our relatives on both sides, and at a joyous Halloween party, we had our usual parade and food festival, and formally welcomed Courtney into the family as our daughter.

Since she had already changed her name from *Une Yung Lee* to *Courtney Child*, she decided to keep her name. "Two names are enough," she said. She did her best to move into her new life and within a year Courtney was calling Paul and me Mom and Dad.

CHAPTER THIRTY-EIGHT

Pequod

Paul was asked to be on the transition team for our newly elected governor Ed King. While in the process, he met Peter Poland, a tall, handsome, and charming man, who'd been a popular political fundraiser in two presidential campaigns. Peter was brilliant, had a Harvard Business School degree, and could sell a toothpick to a toothless man. When he insisted on being Paul's business partner, Paul pondered the idea for a couple of days, and then decided they'd be a good match. Paul specifically asked me to weigh in, and I agreed.

Paul loved *Moby Dick* and with both names as such (Paul Pimentel and Peter Poland), they decided to call the company *Pequod*. Together Paul and Peter were a winning combination, and the first thing they did was to buy a broken-down power plant in New Hampshire with a plan to restore it and sell electricity. Paul was to do the engineering, design work, and management, and Peter was to market it and secure investors.

One day in the early 1980s while making dinner and listening to the 6 o'clock news on TV, I heard Peter's name. I wasn't shocked until I heard the newscaster say Peter had been arrested by FBI agents for involvement in a drug deal. It took my breath away.

I thought, *Peter has everything he needs to be successful. He's obnoxious at times, but he's just too smart to get into such a mess. How could he do such a stupid thing?*

A penetrating nausea came over me; everything we had was on the line—our house, our future, our kids' college educations—everything. I hoped it was all a mistake, but it was all too true.

When Peter went to jail, he left a backlog of bills and several signed and potential engineering contracts; investors had been lined up to support the power plant.

Paul Guzzi called almost immediately. He'd taken a job as a senior executive in a major computer company after leaving his government position. "Pudge, you've got to change the name of your company, and if you can't see this through financially, you should file for bankruptcy; nobody will invest in your power plant now."

"No, I won't do that," Paul answered sharply. "*I've* done nothing *wrong*, and if there are financial ramifications, I'll deal with them. Bankruptcy is *not* an option. I won't carry bankruptcy with me for the rest of my life—it's a sentence I don't deserve."

Paul wanted his association with Peter to end, and was willing to take the consequences to establish a clean separation. So he took the backlog of business and the debt, while Peter took the power plant, sold it, and used the proceeds for his defense. Peter clearly got the better end of the deal, but that was the end of it.

After the Pequod disaster, the days quickly turned into months and then years. The early '80s were gone, and before we knew it the '90s were upon us.

It took more than ten years for Paul's company to get back on track—and in the first five we had learned to live on as little money as possible. We cut costs wherever we could. Five haircuts at the hairdresser's would have been very expensive. So, we five women in the house draped ourselves face-down across the kitchen bar with our heads hanging over the edge so Paul could layer our hair to resemble Farah Fawcett's. Every hair was cut very precisely; engineers make notable hairdressers. And Christopher's mullet was very chic thanks to Paul.

During these difficult times we were always the last in the company to get paid, and there were times when we needed to cover the payroll with loans. Sometimes, *we* didn't get paid at all, generating debt instead of income. But we had great friends and our house was alive with music—and the occasional parade.

Outwardly, everything "appeared" fine, but I still hid my depression deep in my core; my anxiety created a gap between my children and me. Usually, they knew exactly how I would respond. What they didn't know was that my response was related to a pervasive, anxiety-based depression. Paul and the children had no idea, so they never took me seriously; and when I was being my neurotic self, they dismissed my concerns. Life went on.

CHAPTER THIRTY-NINE

Our Italian Daughter

In 1991 our daughter Susan and I joined Paul in Seal Beach, California while he was building an office there for Pequod. I had accumulated weeks of vacation time. So we decided to take advantage of the southern California weather, the beach, and the apartment with its pool and Jacuzzi. For Susan it was like "dying and going to heaven."

While in Seal Beach, Susan befriended a young woman named Valentina. She and her mother Marisa and father Donato lived in the same apartment complex while he was working as an engineer on a special project for Al Italia. Their family lived in Rome, but their roots were in a small town on the Adriatic side of Abruzzo called Bomba, where they co-owned an old manor and other property with relatives.

Susan and Valentina became great friends during our stay. They enjoyed staying up late, partying, and basking in the sun by the pool during the day.

At the end of the Al Italia project, Donato and Marisa went back to Italy; Valentina came back to Massachusetts with Susan for a week-long vacation and stayed a year, becoming our "Italian daughter." By this time Paul and I had mentored many foster children and were quite used to additional teenagers in the house.

Valentina was an older, lighter, and happier version of a similar experience. We loved having this delightful young Italian woman of nineteen with us and assured her worried parents in Italy during regular phone calls that they had nothing to worry about. "We'll watch out for Valentina and she'll be part of our family for as long as she's with us," we assured them.

She was too young to drink legally in America, but did it anyway, and she loved to party. When in *Rome*, do as the *Romans* do. When in *America*, do as the *Romans* do. It was a wild year in the Pimentel house.

Valentina spoke little English when she came to us in 1990; it took her only a few months living in our house to become fluent. When she returned to Italy in 1991 she became a marketable tour guide with a comprehensive command of the English language. In addition she had an incredible grasp of history—a winning combination.

Valentina as a student in Italy

CHAPTER FORTY

Therein Lies Happiness

For more than ten years my gynecologist had suspected I might be suffering from hypothyroidism. It wouldn't have been surprising because we had thyroid disease in the family. As a child, I'd had symptoms that caused my family doctor to question as well, but my thyroid function tests had always come back negative.

In 1993, I heard about a well-respected endocrinologist, Dr. Manfred Ernesti, who was thought to be a genius. So, I made an appointment. When his daughter—his receptionist—guided me into his office I heard him telling a young medical resident to look *closely* at patients during office visits. "See her eyes—they say a lot," he explained to the young Boston medical resident taking a photograph of my face.

Dr. Ernesti was a handsome, flamboyant, middle-aged Brazilian man, and he made me chuckle as he spoke dramatically in an accent that could have been mistaken for Italian. He actually *had* lived in Italy and could speak the language fluently.

Dr. Ernesti was likable and an almost whimsical character, but it quickly became clear that he hadn't acquired his reputation accidently. When the extensive testing was completed, Dr. Ernesti handed me a document and said, "If anyone ever tells you again that your thyroid is normal, show them these test results."

Shortly after the diagnosis of hypothyroidism I had a pan hysterectomy (uterus, tubes—and most importantly—ovaries were removed.) I had been bleeding dangerously and was anemic. After the operation I was placed on a stable regimen of hormone therapy. Getting my hormones in balance has made all the difference.

Not until after this surgery did I realize I'd been depressed for most of my life. Anxiety had held me tightly; it had been there all along "hiding in plain sight."

Due to the hysterectomy and hormone therapy, something wonderful happened—I got happier. Within days my mood had elevated; I'd never experienced organic happiness, the kind that comes with having a balanced chemistry. For the first time, happiness was my natural state of mind; I no longer had to plot against myself or be immersed in music or a parade to feel joy.

Chapter Forty-One

Berkley Circle Turnaround

Our house on Berkley Circle had been a twenty-year experiment in perseverance. We had survived the cold and heat while Paul had become an expert in energy engineering. We had braved complex problems related to our children, our foster children, and two grandchildren.

By 1994 Paul and I decided we were ready for a different style of living. My mother had dropped by the week before when we weren't home and told us later, "I didn't recognize anyone at the dining room table when I opened the door and peeked in, so I left."

We were ready for some peace and to be rid of the responsibility of our house. So we rented the goddamned house at a bargain price to the kids and moved out.

In the winter we bought a cute little condo in Quincy near my office, and decided to live the simple life while our children took care of the house. When we left and moved into the condo, the first thing the kids did was to move the piano out of the den and into the living room so they could create music day and night. We were thrilled to be free of the chores and upkeep demands. It was a *win/win*.

During the year we were in Quincy an awful thing happened. Lisa called one day to tell me that I'd better come over quickly because Courtney was really sick. When I arrived I brought her immediately to the hospital and she was ready for surgery within the hour. Courtney had suffered a stroke when a cerebral aneurism ruptured. By then she was twenty-five and had a five-year-old, our grandson Alexander. She and Alex had been living in the house.

As Paul and I stood next to her while she waited to go to the operating room, she asked "What will happen to my boy?" There was little desperation but extreme sadness in her voice. "I just want to be with my boy and I may never see him again." The emotion was quietly palpable and Paul and I were overwhelmed by the weight of it.

I tried to offer Courtney reassurance, but we both knew it was hollow. This kind of surgery usually doesn't end well. We waited anxiously while Courtney was in surgery. Our friends and family members came in and out of the waiting room to offer support. Joanie stayed with Alex. Our stalwart friends, the Goldbergs, Dands, and Langs stayed with us until it was over.

When the surgeon came into the waiting room, we were all aware of the dismal possibilities and waited quietly. "It went well," he said. He then outlined what he had done to clamp the vessel. He didn't offer much more in terms of her prognosis, and we were afraid to ask.

When Courtney was discharged from the hospital she came to our apartment in Quincy before returning to Hingham. Her physical recovery seemed to go well, but otherwise, she struggled. The whole family rose to the occasion.

It had taken about a year for our children to realize that taking care of a house was a big responsibility, and living together had gotten more difficult for them as well. We decided to move back to our house on Berkley Circle in 1995 and our children decided to get their own places and move on to new adventures.

Chapter Forty-Two

Old Horizons Made New

By 1995 Paul's company was stable enough for us to take a significant vacation. We decided it was time to visit Italy.

Valentina had become the event manager for the *Hassler Hotel* in Rome, and when we asked her to help us plan an Italian trip, she was thrilled. "Don't worry about a thing. I'll plan your entire trip to Italy for the best possible price."

Valentina sent us a detailed and comprehensive itinerary for a five-week trip across Italy. First, a four-day visit with her family and a tour—then we'd drive to my family's town of Prezza in L'Aquila, Abruzzi.

Our trip would then take us to Florence and back across Italy, with stops on our way to and from Venice. The last two weeks we would be without an itinerary. We wanted to travel along the Amalfi coast and visit Positano and Sorrento before returning to Rome and then home to Boston.

The night our flight landed in Rome, Valentina was waiting for us. Like most Italians in Rome she drove like an insane person and I cowered on the floor of the car. Excited at the prospect of us seeing it for the first time, she drove straight to the Coliseum. The breadth of the ancient structure, fully lit in the darkness of the night filled me with awe—it was surreal.

By the time she dropped us off at a lovely hotel we were very tired—but not too tired to marvel at the frescos on the ceilings in the dining room. Our room was simple, yet elegant, and the smell of old wood was familiar to me.

We slept in the next morning. When we opened the shutters, Rome greeted us—the bells rang out as the warm sunlight shown over the rooftops; Saint Peter's Basilica stood majestically in the distance—Sunday morning in Rome.

After seeing every glorious site in the city and the dead Popes, we met Valentina's family at dusk in the middle of Rome at Piazza Navona. Valentina's father Donato insisted on taking us out for the evening. As we lingered at our table, the stars came out and Italian music filled the air—lovely.

The following evening at their apartment, her mother Marisa made us delicious Bolognese pasta and we met Donatella, Valentina's sister. Donato kept insisting that Paul drink grappa after he had consumed too much wine and food—we loved that day.

After our visit, we rented a car and left for Prezza. We were to stay in Sulmona, the historic city of about 25,000 that sits in the valley below the little hill town where my family comes from. I had heard about it over the years and was excited that Valentina had made arrangements for us to stay there. It is best known for its rich history and wedding "confetti"—sugar coated almonds that have become popular for special events. [16]

Aunt Betty had described the road up the hill to Prezza as treacherous. She had maneuvered her large Cadillac up the narrow road during her first trip to Italy and said it was like a suicide run. When Paul drove into the first hairpin turn, I held onto the seat and closed my eyes.

In the village, in a small piazza, men were sitting and chatting. Their faces were familiar to me, especially their eyes—almond-shaped and dark.

When Paul and I stopped and asked the men if they knew my father's cousin Giovanni, they all smiled and quickly directed us upward to a lovely condo complex near the top of the hill overlooking the valley. Their enthusiasm gave us the impression that Giovanni was well liked.

---

16 http://www.made-in-italy.com/italian-food/news/confetti-and-bomboniere-wedding-favors

Aunt Betty and Uncle Jim had visited Prezza in the 1960s. She'd said that a goat had been running through the kitchen of the old mansion that had been part of the family estate when my great great grandfather Nunzio was a wealthy businessman, land owner, and the mayor of the town. This was not the Casa Vecchio (the old house) that Aunt Betty had described, but rather a row of condos that looked more like an upscale apartment complex in San Francisco.

The Casa Vecchio, 1995. Earthquakes led to
its demolition shortly thereafter.

Giovanni greeted us with smiles, hugs, and great warmth. Around him were other family members.

In Prezza: Mario, the baby, Rosella, Maria Grazia,
Giovanni, Sandy; SEATED: Mira

Every expression and line on Giovanni's face was familiar to
me, and his sister Marietta had eyes just like mine. The family
commented on the similarity and said they remembered Aunt Betty
also had the same eyes. The table was covered with homemade
food, and a very special prosciutto that had been cured locally.
"Mangia, mangia," Giovanni insisted. When we were full, I said
the few words I knew at the time; *basta, basta, grazzi—enough,
thank you.*

Giovanni Faiella, Arnaldo, Paul, Domenico

My grandfather Sabatino's sister Micarosa's grandson Arnaldo took us to the town cemetery and the familiar names and the pictures on the gravestones looked like relatives in the Point. We found the names Faiella, Sandonado, Spadorcia, and Pasquale throughout the graveyard. The glass-covered photographs imbedded in the gravestones strongly resembled my relatives and those I had seen in Quincy where people from Prezza had ventured to find work; the men looked like my father, and the women like my aunts.

On the day we left Prezza, my relatives gathered and gave us bottles of local wine and sugar coated almonds from Sulmona. We went on to complete the remarkable trip that Valentina had prepared for us—Florence, Sienna, Venice, and a beautiful monastery on the top of a hill in Tuscany where we watched the sun set over a storm in the valley—it was a magnificent sight.

Chapter Forty-Three

Reconciliation

In the mid-1990s, Paul's business had required him to be on the road a great deal. His sisters Susan and Joan lived in California and Florida. This left Fred alone much of the time and he was slowing down. I felt compelled to keep an eye on him in the absence of his children.

At that point I was working in the District Attorney's Office in Dedham, and daily, I drove through Braintree on my way home to Hingham. It was easy for me to pick him up something for dinner or to drop by and chat for a while. He'd become more pleasant in his old age and he seemed appreciative of the company. I always worried that I wasn't watching closely enough.

On a cold winter's night I turned the corner onto Arnold Street and saw flashing blue lights. I held my breath. A wonderful neighbor had checked in on him and called 911.

Fred had fallen in the garage the day before and had been lying on the cold cement floor since. Fortunately the frigid temperatures of the week before had risen above freezing, but it was still very cold. I felt a surge of guilt and profound sadness when I saw the ambulance staff lift him up into the vehicle. He was listless and confused and there was a bump on his head that indicated he had fallen. It was an awful scene.

Fred was in the hospital for several days and he ultimately went to a rehab center and then to a nursing home, where we expected him to recover and then return home. Several weeks later I received a call from the nursing home. Fred had been sent to the emergency room in critical condition. Paul was away on business and his sisters were thousands of miles away. Fred had given me a rough time for many years, and now, ironically, I was the one to be contacted about his well-being.

When I met him in the ER we both knew he was dying. I sensed his annoyance that it was I and not his children standing next to him. I didn't blame him. "I'll get you home Grandpa, I promise—I know it's what you want."

Fred shook his head—his contempt for me obvious; he had allowed me to help him in the absence of his family in the previous year or two, and we had, in fact, developed a way of bantering that was almost fun, but in his most vulnerable state I felt the truth.

I called Paul and his sisters to tell them that they didn't have much time to get home. They all made immediate arrangements and were underway within the day. I called Hospice. By the time the meeting was set, my sister-in-law Joanie was there to take over. She was the expert in such things, a nurse and the director of a Hospice in California.

When Fred's family surrounded the bed set up in the living room of their family home in Braintree, his breathing was quiet and shallow. The nurse said he'd refused medication and was fully aware of what was happening; the most a dying man could hope is to die in his own home with his children and grandchildren around him.

I hung back—he only wanted his blood around him—nothing had changed in that regard. It wasn't my place to be next to him and I didn't really want to be there.

Everyone encouraged me to move closer. So I did, and touched his arm gently. He clenched his hand—and I stepped back. At that point in our lives, I no longer felt the need to be in his favor—psychologically or otherwise. I watched Fred leave his world knowing I'd done my best for him in spite of our rocky relationship. I was at peace with it.

Fred, in his last days, had finally accepted the daughter and granddaughter he had kept at bay during the time he was caring for his wife Dorothy. She'd passed away with Alzheimer's disease several years earlier after he battled with God to keep her alive for many years. When she was gone, he was left with the prospect of a lonely life of isolation. When Dorothy died, the last vestige of Fred's control went with her. He had no friends other than the neighbors whom he had hired to help with Dorothy, and he was confronted with the reality of his empty life.

While Fred lived, he battled with the devil. He was a religious man, who, for many years, couldn't listen to his God. I likened him to my own grandfather Geoffrey who waited too long. They were both stubborn and rigid, and their bigotry paralyzed them.

When Fred finally came around, it was easy. It was difficult not to be captivated by Rachel who was a delightful child with a smiling face and big loving eyes. When Fred finally met her, he was hooked. But for her bi-racial complexion, she looked just like him. Fred was helpless.

I was happy for Rachel and in knowing that Fred had experienced the joy of her before his death. My heart always ached for her father Kirby who never showed disdain for Fred in spite of having been marginalized. Kirby and I were, in many ways, kindred spirits, outsiders who could never breach the wall of family.

My father-in-law was surrounded by the few people he had allowed into his life, his children—Paul, Susan, and Joan— our children, and Rachel. As they all stood around his bed, our youngest daughter Joanie sang "Amazing Grace," as only she can, while little Rachel held Fred's hand. He was indeed a lucky man.

PART 5

CHAPTER FORTY-FOUR

A Dream Comes True

Anthony DiBenedetto was impressed with work done by Pequod. When his company was acquired, he strongly recommended that Paul's company be considered for acquisition as well. Pequod was made a substantial offer and in 1996 Paul sold his company, pleased to need never again worry about meeting payroll.

Following the sale of the company we became close friends with the DiBenedetto family; Anthony resembles my father's siblings and the Italian connection made us likely paesanos; Anthony and Eileen are now very close friends.

The first thing we did after the sale was to renovate the core of our solar house, making it larger and adding a huge screened-in porch. I loved sitting in the fresh air on summer nights. On Sunday mornings our daughters and their husbands and our grandchildren frequently came over for brunch. We loved it.

Two years after the company sold, Paul and I began thinking about our long-term plans. We had always dreamed about buying a house on Martha's Vineyard. In 1999, we purchased a house on the island large enough to accommodate our friends and family. We were both still working so we couldn't go to "the Vineyard" as often as we would have liked, but we knew that one day we would live there—and in the meantime, we would enjoy it when we could.

CHAPTER FORTY-FIVE

Work

I had changed jobs numerous times over the years. Before working for Bill Delahunt in 1986, I'd held a variety of positions with the Massachusetts Department of Mental Health (DMH): as an aftercare nurse; a case manager; and then with chronically mentally ill people in a day treatment center. While working at Boston City Hospital, I ran an outreach team that provided interventions designed to keep students in school as part of a Robert Wood Johnson Foundation research grant to study absenteeism and truancy. The team was located in a school that was surrounded by public housing developments that had been the hotbed of racial tensions during Boston's desegregation.

During my tenure in the DA's office, I'd designed and managed education, advocacy, and community programs to support victims of domestic violence, homicide, elder abuse, and the like, with a focus on prevention programs in schools. While I always had a flair in the community, and could help victims, I lacked the knowledge of the legal process.

It took me too long to connect the dots in the DAs office, and at times, I put myself out there before I was ready. I hadn't yet learned the importance of asking questions and I didn't listen to the masters soon enough. I think that my depression made it difficult to put my ego aside. This is something I will always regret. Damn it all, why didn't I know better?

By the time Bill Delahunt was elected to congress I was grounded, seasoned, and experienced. By the time Bill Keating became District Attorney, I'd learned a great deal and my experience allowed me to be far more effective in my job.

CHAPTER FORTY-SIX

Bridges to Islam

Bill Keating was elected DA in 1999 and I worked with him until 2003 when I retired. My last project before retirement was in response to Bill's request to establish a relationship and program with the Islamic Center of New England in Quincy to negate mistrust and to promote understanding. It was my job to open and maintain communication.

Through a friend I was introduced to the Imam's wife Hind, and she introduced me to her husband, Imam Talal Eid who agreed to let me meet with women in the mosque. We created a monthly women's group that I called, "Ladies of the Mosque." As the organizer and facilitator of the group of eight women who gathered together, I listened carefully as they freely shared their views and perspectives and talked about their faith. I learned a lot and came to appreciate these women.

To help me understand the culture, the Imam provided me with explanations in writing. About half the women in the group were college educated, and all wore the *hijab* and clothing common to women in this Mosque. They told me their style of dress is comfortable for a number of reasons that are both practical and personal, and a way to separate their public and private lives.

I was honest with them, and in time, they came to know that we at the DA's office had their best interests at heart. Mutual respect went a long way to promote understanding.

In time the Imam began calling me "Miss Sandy," and we worked to secure a collaborative grant to fund a local workshop to unify the community. Part of my job was to sit on the Quincy Human Rights Commission and to work with the Mayor's Commission on Women. This strengthened the collaboration.

About a year later on a beautiful fall morning, I was rocking on my front porch on Martha's Vineyard. I rested my head back and gentle gusts of warm air touched my face. It was indeed a glorious day.

When the phone rang I was annoyed but I've never been very good at letting a phone call pass. When I answered, my mother greeted me, crying. "There's been a terrible attack in New York City, turn on your television!" I flipped the knob and just as the picture focused, the second plane hit the World Trade Center.

During the following week in Quincy there was a citywide gathering of hundreds of people in the stadium. Being out of town was frustrating, but I was enormously relieved to learn the Imam would stand in solidarity on the stage with the other clergy. I hoped our work in bringing him into the community network had made a difference in this outcome; the police and other officials had been working with us during the previous months, and my sense was that it improved the dynamic in the community.

September 11, 2001— *Life as we'd known it would never be the same.*

Two days after the attack on the World Trade Center our family was bound for Washington DC. Paul was to receive an award at the White House from the Department of Energy for a design that he had built. He convinced me that it was the safest time to fly. We were the only ones on the plane. Because of security issues in Washington, Paul was honored in a government building in a remote part of the city.

In the following year my work continued at the Mosque. On December 9, 2002, the Islamic Center of New England, the Norfolk District Attorney's Office, the Quincy Human Rights Commission, the National Conference for Communities and Justice, and the Quincy Police Department sponsored a coffee hour and education forum. Our plans finally had come to fruition.

The enthusiasm and variety of backgrounds and professions of the participants and representatives made it a unique event.

Of all my interaction with the "Ladies of the Mosque," I most cherish having been invited to the Imam's daughter's wedding in Lebanon. Though I couldn't attend, I deeply appreciated the special trust that had developed between us.

Bridges are built far more easily when trust is the common denominator.

CHAPTER FORTY-SEVEN

Berkley Circle Sale

We spent several more peaceful years at our Berkley Circle solar home in Hingham. In the years between 1994 and 2003, we'd enjoyed Sunday morning brunches, birthday parties, weddings, anniversary parties—the usual. But, it was time for Paul and me to move on.

Of all of the things I would miss about Berkley Circle, the parades took top billing. They occurred regularly—and our grandchildren, when they reached their teens—grew to be embarrassed by them. But they couldn't help themselves—they participated, too.

Our daughter Lisa managed to become a member of the Roma Band of the North End. At that time she was the only woman to play and march with them. When Lisa became friends with all the old, Italian musicians, they'd started coming to parties at our house. I'd feed them pasta and they always brought big jugs of home-made red wine and would joke that white wine was for the weak or Protestants.

Roma Band playing at a holiday celebration in our living room

Some of the band members were in their eighties and accustomed to marching around the North End in the summer heat for hours. At Christmas time, on dark cold nights, they'd march along Berkley Circle and stop at various houses to play along the way. We wondered how these elderly guys could still stand after consuming so much alcohol. Fortunately young band members were always available to drive them back to Boston after our parties.

Marching along Berkley Circle at Christmas

They enjoyed life and loved to tease. When Guy, the bandleader called our house looking for Lisa, I'd pretend she didn't live with us anymore. He'd then ask, "Where is she—in jail?"

Our last holiday in Hingham was the Fourth of July. The Roma Band had been hired to march in the local parade. Paul and I had attended every year for decades. Twenty years before, we'd watch with our children, and later with our grandchildren, ending the day with a cook-out at the Goldbergs' house nearby. It was always a great day for us.

On this day, we could hear the undisciplined sound of the brass and drums of the Roma Band approaching—charmingly unmistakable. As Sal and our old Italian friends moved closer, we waved and caught their attention. When they reached us, they turned and clustered around us.

We felt like dignitaries in a reviewing stand. They began to play my father's favorite song—"O Sole Mio." I felt a lump in my throat knowing that this would be our last Hingham parade with them. The entire parade had come to a halt and other bands and floats had backed up in the delay. But our friends didn't care; they just kept playing. As embarrassing as it was, we loved it—and them.

Billy Flynn, Lisa, and other members of The
Roma Band playing in our living room

While the years in the Berkley Circle house had been wonderful, we had had our share of the heartaches that occur in most families. When the house sold, our children and grandchildren felt like they'd lost an old friend. Paul and I felt for them, but we were so excited to move on to our next chapter.

We secured a beautiful 5th floor condo in the North End overlooking Boston Harbor. As this was the area where my grandparents Sabatino and Emma had begun their relationship, the neighborhood had a certain familiarity that made us feel at home.

Paul loved the North End and attempted to eat in all of the 101 restaurants that offered superb Italian cuisine. I loved hanging out at Mike's Pastry and eating cannolis on Saturday mornings, or listening to the banter of the Italians who meandered along Hanover Street on a warm summer's night. We both got fat.

While we loved living in the North End, we slowly began to spend more time in our house on Martha's Vineyard. By the end of the second year in Boston, we were ready to move to the island permanently.

I was convinced there could be no better place for us than the island. Arriving at the ferry in Woods Hole after our various travels, we were often jet lagged and tense. While traveling is wonderful, it's also stressful. Coordinating it all with the ferry schedule can add to it. But, when we arrived at the pier, the sun would be approaching the horizon, and the ferry departed just in time to see the sky turn pink. Paul and I could feel our stress defuse in the salty air.

When we finally arrived at our house, we'd fall into bed, feeling as if we were on another planet. The following morning we drank coffee on the deck and enjoyed the peacefulness. While some might long for the energy of the city, the island was the perfect spot for Paul and me.

It really was time to move. Paul's company had been sold yet again, and he was part of the deal. When he said he wanted to retire, the new company offered him the opportunity to set up his office on the Vineyard—and in our house—if that was his choice. That *was* his choice.

Though, in the ensuing years, the company was sold twice again, Paul continues as the Senior Vice President of Engineering for an international energy service company that designs and modifies efficient power plants and buildings.

Creative, artistic, and interesting people keep life vibrant and meaningful for us here; friendships are often deep and loyal, and we've learned to see the world as our neighborhood and our island as our extended family. Our house isn't ostentatious, but it's large enough to accommodate our children, grandchildren, and friends, who love to come whenever they can.

I had always said that in order to be happy with financial stability we needed to be happy without it. We had faced financial challenges and assumed that everything would be fine—so, everything *was* fine. We lived like my Italian relatives who danced to the music while everyone worried about the ship going down; we always knew that the ship could and would be repaired before disaster struck, and believed that life would work out—and it did.

CHAPTER FORTY-EIGHT

Full Circle

We'd thought about Frank and Julius over the years and had wondered about Julius's survival, hoping that he'd rallied in Detroit in the aftermath of the trauma in Wynton. Though we were a long time and space from those very difficult days, Frank and Julius still were tucked in the back of our minds.

When our old and dear friends, Judy and Cliff Genge told us about meeting a woman who'd been at the pub on the night Frank and Julius were shot, it had all rushed back to us.

She told them that while the boys had been playing pool someone recognized the ring on Frank's finger and knew it had come from the jewelry store robbery. When Frank realized the ring had been noticed, he pulled a gun out of his jacket, and the ring flipped onto the floor.

Frank pointed the gun at a woman and threatened her as he insisted that she retrieve the ring. Terrified, she found it and gave it to him. Frank backed away toward the door and Julius followed. They moved quickly toward their car hoping to escape, but when Frank attempted to start the engine, it flooded. They then jumped out and ran toward the woods. Reportedly, Frank and Julius tried to escape over a mound and into the relative cover of the trees beyond. While they headed for the woods, a group of patrons retrieved guns and rifles from their trucks and cars.

By that time Frank had reached the wooded area. Julius was an easy target as he reached the crest of the hill. As the shooters on the porch discharged their weapons again and yet again, ammunition from a 12-gauge shotgun, a 22 rifle, and from numerous weapons sprayed into Julius's back. His arms flailed as he fell to the ground with a pulsating thump. The woman had described the gunfire as intense and persistent.

When Frank saw that his brother had been shot, he pulled out a white handkerchief and waved it high in surrender. It was then that the crowd shifted their attention to Frank and continued their shooting spree. In spite of the considerable distance, one of the shots managed to shatter Frank's right elbow.

The woman had told them it was like being in an arcade and that the shooters were laughing. The foliage on the mound had been entirely cut to the ground by bullets; even small trees had been completely severed.

Frank turned and fled deeper into the woods. When he reached the highway and the phone booth, he called me, and subsequently I met him there.

The rest of what the woman had said about Frank and Julius—and additionally—about us—was truly ugly. She finished by saying, "Those niggers got their due in the end, and I hope those pinko liberals learned their lesson, too."

When Frank had begun to decompensate, he'd lost all sense of reality. His actions were careless, and at times, almost bizarre. In later years I realized that much of Frank's behavior was driven by mental illness, and that he was more than likely bipolar. He died when he was barely thirty years old. I never knew the cause.

Julius, on the other hand, had had the "audacity of hope." But it came too late, a sad reality. I often wondered if the lead bullet left near his heart played havoc in the course of his life. Julius died in his early fifties.

There'd been a perfect storm in Wynton. Frank had unleashed the mob with due force, and our naïveté and intent to make a difference had profoundly impacted the future of both those young men; there isn't much redemption in what happened in Wynton.

I found solace in knowing that while Frank and Julius had been thieves, they never stole even a dime from us, and in spite of overwhelming odds, they didn't use drugs. During the time Frank and Julius lived with us, I learned the importance of having a job, and how difficult it is to find one when you don't have privilege. My instincts had been right in many ways, but I had had no idea about the world; they gave back what they'd been given, and survival was all they knew. Perhaps there's a lesson somewhere in the entirety of this picture—perhaps.

Chapter Forty-Nine

Let the Construction Begin

In 2014 we had a cedar barn built. While functional, it's also beautiful. The first story has an open plan and the loft is large enough for parties and sleeping. The sun-warmed cedar serves as aroma-therapy on any spring day. Paul designed it, and a lovely Amish family from Pennsylvania came to build it.

Ephraim Riehl, the father of the young men on the construction team, made the arrangements with us by phone and post as there could be no emails or electronic contacts because of their religious beliefs.

Pre-cut beams and planks arrived on trucks via the ferry, and within hours, the skeleton of the building was sitting on a cement slab that had been perfectly poured to accommodate the structure.

I held my breath as Ephraim's sons maneuvered across open beams like they were promenading on the beach. I fed them whenever they needed food, and when one of them got sick, I offered him a bed and plenty of fluids.

The young men were always graciously quiet while letting the eldest, Elmer, do the talking. He was tall and lanky and wore a wide-brimmed hat. All the brothers had bowl haircuts, and the one young man who was married had a beard. His wife had just had a baby son; the women hadn't come to the Island because of the baby's age.

When the barn was completed it was solid and impressive. Every joint fit perfectly, the beams were massive, and it was exactly what we had asked them to build. We were thrilled with it.

We had a clambake at the end of the week to show our appreciation, and they all ate lobster for the first time. Paul had fun teaching them to dissect every morsel of meat from the shells. He always gets excited when the opportunity arises for him to supervise. And if people get impatient with the little legs or the bodies, he's always there to clean and eat them himself.

Of course, we installed solar panels. We had already bought a generator, a new heat pump, and an electric car—we were ready for the new millennium—it's unlikely I'll ever see my breath again *inside* on Christmas morning.

When it came time for the Amish family to go home, I carefully asked, "Are you allowed to give hugs?" I was happy when each of the boys gave me a careful embrace, and when they came several weeks later to do another job on the other side of the Island, they came by to say *hello* and to introduce us to their wives and the newest member of the family. It was then I realized they really were friends, if only for a moment in time.

Chapter Fifty

The Net Result

The years passed quickly—too quickly. By the time Paul and I had been married for fifty years we'd put our difficult times behind us. Paul had experienced war, financial disaster at the hands of an unscrupulous partner, cancer, quadruple bypass surgery, two bouts of septicemia, Lyme disease, and emergency surgery to remove a large single piece of plaque from his left carotid artery just before it was ready to cause a massive stroke. This is a *very* lucky man; I dare say that my nursing background helped—there were a few times where it made the difference between life and death.

The good news is that Paul is healthy now. He's seventy-three and has danced between life and death while feeling like a warrior king most of the time. His only complaint is that his neck lacks mobility because of the radiation he had in his thirties, and that he needs to take medication to prevent gout—not bad for an old man.

CHAPTER FIFTY-ONE

The Legacy Goes On

Reflecting on life at this age is not unusual. We were in a great place and we marveled that we'd made it. We wondered how the chaos of life in our house over the years had affected our children and their relationships with us. They were always the kindest kids in the room, but they weren't always easy. I often wondered when I received Christmas cards from people who wrote about their perfect children if they were being honest—we didn't have perfect children and sometimes they were awful. There were times when I wondered if I was the worst mother in the world, but then something wonderful happened—*they grew up!*

Lisa graduated from the University of Massachusetts in Amherst. She's been a music teacher for more than two decades. Lisa sees the wonder in every child. She uses music masterfully to promote positive social change and teaches children that it takes hard work to succeed—and they know she's telling the truth.

Lisa's gifts are appreciated. A single parent living on the edge once told me of her child's transformation because of Lisa's ability to motivate him; the mother of a Yale student told me that Lisa had been her son's second grade teacher and that he'd written about her in his college application essay; an academy award-winning actor told Paul and me how much our daughter had influenced his children.

While teaching has served as her primary career, Lisa has become a seasoned songwriter, producer, and performer. She plays various instruments, sings, and like her grandfather Panfilio, the *world* is her *stage*.

Lisa is step-mother to her husband Bob's children, Emily and Christopher, and they have two grandchildren Brooklyn and Blaydie.

When Christopher was six, he had difficulty learning to read. Somewhere along the way his brain switched into learning mode and he blossomed. In his late twenties he read Nietzsche for fun.

Chris graduated from the University of Colorado with distinction in his field. He received his law degree from Suffolk Law School in Boston and passed the bar on his first try. Of all his accomplishments his ability to parent is the most impressive—he's a wonderful father and his children adore him. Chris is married to beautiful Karen and they have two children, a boy and a girl—Mitchell and Sage.

Though Christopher is a lawyer, he's an entrepreneur at heart, and like his father, he's always thinking and *connecting dots*. While working in a technology licensing office as an Assistant Agreements Specialist at Massachusetts General Hospital, Chris approached the principal investigators in the photochemical tissue bonding lab with a proposal to enter their technology in the MIT 50K Entrepreneurship Competition (now called the 100K.) The scientists liked the idea and agreed to move forward. In short they were one of five finalists to be chosen and he received an award from the premier startup competition in the world at that time.

When Susan was in the third grade she wrote a poem that serves as a metaphor for her life.

If I were the King of the World, what would I do?
I'd make love and joy and peace for all.
I'd run carnivals every day.
I'd get rid of atomic bombs
And all the things I don't understand.
I'd make kids the boss and parents the followers.
I'd grow flowers.
I'd make everyone happy
Or try at least.
I'd be friends with everyone
And I'd give to the poor.
I'd stop wars
And make peace.
That's what I'd do.

Susan's job is outlined in her poem—for many years she's worked in one of the most notorious and challenged inner cities in the country with uncommon success as a marriage and family therapist and program manager. She understands privilege and works to level the playing field every day. She learned to run civil rights and violence-prevention workshops right out of high school. In her early twenties, she traveled to Guatemala as an activist and peace worker with others from UMASS Boston.

Susan has learned to make *the sauce* like Grandma Emma and creativity shines through her life. She lives with her husband Chris and their two children, Isabella and Augustus.

Joanie is a fearless and loyal warrior who never hesitates to stand up for the underdog or for what she believes is right. She once received a late night phone call for defending two innocent young black friends in the press—the man on the phone threatened to kill her and called her—well you can imagine what he called her. It was a terrifying time.

While music has always been part of Joanie's life, she's also used her considerable technical and artistic gifts over the years; before venturing into a full-time career in music she led a graphics production team in a national retail company.

Joanie has much to be proud of. She writes, records, and performs music and has received several music awards over the years. Her exquisite singing voice has brought her to audiences in the United States, Europe, and China, and she is currently a professional performer and teacher of vocal and instrumental music.

Joanie currently lives in California with her husband Rob. As a blended family, Joanie and Rob helped raise three boys, Alex, Anthony, and Erik. The boys have grown into delightful young men.

Courtney is a living miracle—a survivor—a woman who is here by virtue of her willingness to keep trying, and because she never gives up. Every day she fights the fight. She accepts truth with humility and her generosity is often beyond what she has to give.

Whenever I'm having a bad day, I remember the sum total of my children who have grown to be kind and loving people who readily accept everyone. It's then that I know for sure that I've made the world a better place.

CHAPTER FIFTY-TWO

50ᵗʰ Wedding Anniversary

Paul and I knew what we wanted to do for our fiftieth anniversary—we wanted the sum total of our lives in one incredible week.

Our son Christopher found online a magnificent house in Maine that had everything and anything a child or adult could want. We rented it for the week of June 20ᵗʰ, 2015. It sounded too good to be true—it wasn't.

After a long drive, we arrived to see the magnificent vista of the White Mountains. The house had an indoor pool, a movie theater, three hot tubs, spas—it went on and on, and the opulence of it almost embarrassed me.

Our vacation house

The scenes of my childhood resonated every night for a week—the debates, individual and collective performances with guitars and drums, and the children at the center of life moving freely, jumping, hugging, and building memories—like mine on Edwards Street.

In a large room that looked like Hogwarts in the Harry Potter story, there were loyal friends and family, the tolerance of Albion, and the gratitude of survival. It was everything that Paul and I could have ever hoped for, and as we looked at the people we loved we wished that others could understand it all and how it came to be.

Each one of the family prepared something for us. The most touching among them were our adult grandchildren.

Anthony, now twenty-three, started first by admitting that he was a sap and cried openly as he said his piece. Then the others spoke—grandchildren who came to us through marriages and hardships. They too cried. There were twelve of them in total, and several came to us individually to thank us for teaching them about life, and for being there for them and for their parents.

When I think about my relationships with my grandmothers, and compare them to the way I interact with my two oldest grandsons, I realize how much the paradigm has shifted. My relationships with Alex and Anthony are extraordinarily easy and comfortable. They talk freely about what they think, and feel, and love, and are comfortable in letting me know that they're not perfect. As their grandmother, I adore them and they know it. I love that they want to be with me, and in a strange and almost magical way, they are my friends.

Blaydie, our beautiful little five-year old, bi-racial great-grandson, with his copper ringlets and sweet nature, seldom says a word. But on this occasion, he recited a song. This was monumental.

As he stood in the front of the room with Lisa, he summed it all up:

Love grows, one by one
Two by two and four by four
Love grows 'round like a circle
And comes back knocking at your front door.[17]

---

17 Love Grows One by One, Composer: Carol Johnson

Chapter Fifty-Three

A Circle of Acceptance

By some grace or grand plan Paul and I landed in the same place at the same time. Paul saw things in black and white, thought life should be orderly, with little drama or romance. I, on the other hand, was disorganized and creative and spontaneous.

Our family made great sacrifices for Paul's career—he spent hours and hours away from me and from his children—both in body and spirit. In the era of the early years of our marriage, that's what men did if they were to be successful.

When we were young, my mind was consumed with drama that reflected my insecurity. Because Paul had a high IQ, I thought he knew everything. He used that to his advantage when we argued; he would bully me into thinking the problem was mine.

In our middle years together, I was busy raising children, taking in teenage foster children (mostly wounded young girls), and working full-time. In addition, I was engaged in numerous political efforts—I was crazed.

In the midst of the chaos, I finally got up the wherewithal to complete college. I came out feeling I was a capable woman and much smarter than the little girl who cried hard when she saw her first report card. I emerged with a new thirst for thinking and learning.

When the Equal Rights Amendment was on the ballot, the status quo was shaken to its core. Couples of our generation did one of three things in the face of the women's movement: they either kept things the way they were, imploded in divorce, or grew *together* and *through* the changes to a new relationship.

For us it was the last: we were both somehow able to look at ourselves and each other honestly, and learned that mutual and objective introspection is a *must* in a growing and changing relationship. If you're able to face truth, introspection is a marvelous tool, but you come to realize every mistake you ever made—and it isn't easy.

Paul and I have been fortunate. We had grown together rather than apart, and for this I will always be grateful. We weren't always happy together, but in those times when we weren't good for each other, we figured it out—and just as importantly, we stuck it out. In spite of every *goddamned* stupid mistake we ever made, our family and friends have always trusted and accepted us without reservation. In retrospect I have a mindful appreciation of how different life would have been in the absence of unconditional acceptance and love. It has been extraordinary!

END

Sunflowers Reach the Sky

Sandy Pimentel

There are little lines on my face now; my hands are
signed, too.
They're maps of all my days on earth.
The years escape me—one folding into the other, like
chapters in a novel.
As I read the pages, I'm comforted.
I have my family—my husband, and children born of
my body and heart.
Paul learned of the birth of our first child as his ship
moved through the South China Sea. Guns roared.
As I held my baby to my breast, it was difficult to
imagine how life and death could be so much a part of
my world.
The war ended.
We were young and naïve—life's lessons were hard and
painful.
I always found fresh air to dance on my face—I'm
grateful.
We laughed and cried together, and apart;
We cared for each other in light-hearted ways and never
took any problem too seriously, for too long.
Our children grew up—they're almost perfect.
I love to watch them parent; they don't make my
mistakes.
Their babies tickle my soul until it cries.
My children's children were submerged in bugs and
stars and dreams of heroes and princesses;
And as they grow, more children fill the empty spaces.
Through the stream of our lives came the troubled and
the desperate young, looking for hope.

They taught us important lessons about life and the world.

Time brought change; eternity feels like a day.

My body is no longer lean; my Italian genes crave fresh pasta.

I love to prepare plump red tomatoes and black olives bursting with oil.

I long for the smell of dark green basil, and—most of all—garlic.

This is my food and the food of my people.

My trip has been frivolous and fun and fantastic, and I love having friends along for the ride.

As I reach the best part of my life, I am moved by the depth and breadth of it, and in knowing that it will never end.

There'll be more souls while I am here and to follow, and I already love them, for time is one.

Laughter, tears, rage, and hilarious tales have sculpted my soul, and human spirits are all around me—growing, learning, struggling and striving, as they will.

My seasoned hands are held high,
Sunflowers that reach the sky.

My Family Tree

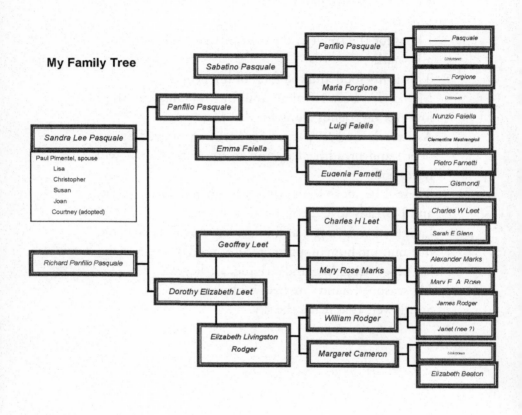

Sandra Lee Pasquale

Paul Pimentel, spouse
  Lisa
  Christopher
  Susan
  Joan
  Courtney (adopted)

Richard Panfilio Pasquale

Panfilio Pasquale

Sabatino Pasquale

Panfilo Pasquale

_____ Pasquale

Unknown

Maria Forgione

_____ Forgione

Unknown

Emma Faiella

Luigi Faiella

Nunzio Faiella

Clementina Mastrangioli

Eugenia Farnetti

Pietro Farnetti

_____ Gismondi

Dorothy Elizabeth Leet

Geoffrey Leet

Charles H Leet

Charles W Leet

Sarah E Glenn

Mary Rose Marks

Alexander Marks

Mary F A Rose

Elizabeth Livingston Rodger

William Rodger

James Rodger

Janet (nee ?)

Margaret Cameron

Unknown

Elizabeth Beaton

My Pasquale Family Tree

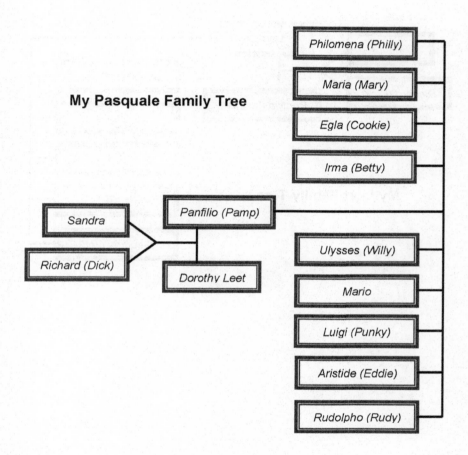

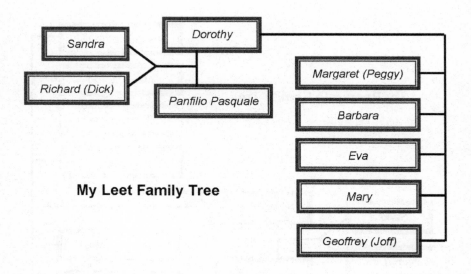

My Leet Family Tree

APPENDIX

IN CELEBRATION
OF MY FAMILY

CHAPTER ONE

My Ancestors

DISCOVERING GENEALOGY

When I reached my late sixties, thinking it would be fun to look at my ancestry, I took up genealogy as a hobby. That hobby led to a journey into my past, and in many ways, into myself.

The exploration of ancestry provides dates and countries and professions and immigration information. But what we really want is to know what motivated people, what they thought, and who they were as human beings. We want to know what they endured, what they achieved, and how they related to the world.

I learned important lessons and filled in some gaps while I was learning. The most profound lesson I learned is that we are descended from imperfect heroes, ordinary people trapped in the standards of their time. I'm grateful for my parents, their parents, and the generation before them who dared to travel to places completely unfamiliar to them.

I've come to respect the risk each of them took to make it possible for me to be *me*. I owe my heroes their day, even if it is twenty, fifty, or a hundred years later. While I can't know to any degree the intimacies of previous generations, I've chosen to share my understanding of what I've discovered with my children and their children and with my readers. I suspect there are many families that resemble mine.

Truth is always difficult to substantiate, especially when looking back more than a century. Accolades tend to get exaggerated with the passage of time, but sometimes it's all we have. For this reason it's important to pass it on so that the next generation can savor it and understand the tenor of where they came from and how they came to be:

My first experience into my past was with my great, great, grandfather Nunzio Faiella, who, I had heard, was the Mayor of Prezza.

CHAPTER TWO

***

Paternal Ancestors

THE FAIELLA FAMILY

My grandmother Emma was born in 1888 in Prezza, a small hill town above Sulmona, in Abruzzi, Italy, and was raised with privilege. Emma's grandfather Nunzio Faiella was the mayor of Prezza and owned olive orchards and a huge villa called the Casa Vecchio—The Old House—where he lived with his wife Maria Clementina (née Mastrangioli).

After becoming a successful businessman in Rome, Nunzio had moved back to Prezza to be with his family. Nonetheless, his business continued to call him to Rome.

On those return trips to the city, the road Nunzio had to travel from Prezza to Sulmona was narrow and difficult. His dray would twist back and forth down the steep hill as his driver negotiated the treacherous hairpin turns. While the coach waiting in Sulmona to take him to Rome was steadier, the ride to the city was always long and tedious, and if the weather was bad, it could take two days.

In the mid-eighteen hundreds, when the railway was being built from Rome to Pescara (on the east coast of Italy), the plan was for a straight shot from west to east. Mayor Nunzio Faiella had had his fill of inconvenient travel. He wielded enough political capital to convince people in Rome to divert the train track up the hill to Prezza and then back down to Sulmona, which made his journeys back and forth faster and considerably more pleasant.

It was the only diversion in the entire track across Italy from the Tyrrhenian Sea in the west to the Adriatic Sea in the east.

The railroad comes to Prezza, thanks to Nunzio

Nunzio Faiella and another of my paternal great, great grandfathers—Pietro Gismondi—were close friends. Pietro was reportedly the designer and manager of the railroad in Prezza. He had gone there to do his work and he often brought his daughter Eugenia Farnetti and her young son Arnaldo with him. Sometimes they would stay with Nunzio's cousin Gaetano, a priest in Prezza. Eugenia had been married in another town several years earlier. I was told several stories about her earlier life—that she was a widow, that she was divorced, that she was unable to divorce—but I could never find the truth with any sense of confidence.

When Eugenia met Nunzio's son Luigi, she was instantly captivated. He was charming and handsome and he was attracted to her as well. They soon fell in love and married.

Nunzio and his son Luigi both embraced her child and, in many ways, this is how life moved forward for more than one hundred years. Little Arnaldo was the first known child to be embraced in my history and he went on to become a successful and loving husband, father, and grandfather. In many ways my story begins with him.

When Nunzio became ill in 1888, his only son Luigi was called back to his bedside from his medical studies in Rome. "Stay in Prezza," Nunzio pleaded, "the business needs you."

Luigi. Born November 28, 1852, Married June 15, 1884   Eugenia (née Farnetti) De Nicola

Nunzio passed away within weeks, and Luigi was left with his father's fortune, and with the responsibility of his businesses.

Luigi and Eugenia had six more children: Elvira, Bianca, Emma, Giselda, Pia, and Rudolpho. They were all healthy until Pia, their two-year-old baby girl, died from a leg injury. After that loss Eugenia became over-protective of her other children.

Luigi did not possess his father's business acumen. Some called him lazy, but he hadn't been groomed to work. As an only child his father had spoiled him, and then sent him to Rome to be educated with the best. When he came home refined and confident, handsome and dignified, Luigi was a man of Rome, and above engaging in menial labor.

As his and Eugenia's family grew, he sat under the olive trees playing cards; business suffered. When he realized his business was failing, he assumed the newly unified Italy was suffering an economic crisis. So he left his olive orchards in Prezza, his Casa Vecchio, and his land to be tended by extended family members and took his wife and children to Minas Gerais, Brazil to begin again while he was still a rich man, possibly to raise coffee.[18]

Sandy and Paul below the Casa Vecchio in 1995

18 http://www.brazil.org.za/minas-gerais.html

Luigi's fortune seemed endless. He had bought boat and train tickets for him and Eugenia, their six children, their thirteen servants—and *their* families without batting an eye. While Luigi's business prowess was "less than wonderful," family lore indicates that he had financed the immigration of many people from Italy to America in the face of economic turmoil. By all reports, he was a very generous man.

They left for Brazil in 1897. Shortly after Luigi and Eugenia arrived at their new home in Minas Gerais, their seventh child, Americo, was born.

Eugenia wore elbow-length gloves and exquisite feathered hats that shaded her shoulders; her daughters wore lace bodices tucked into their floor-length satin skirts cinched with wide belts—the couture of distinguished Italian women in the early 1900s; in rural Brazil, style was not so important.

Four of Luigi and Eugenia Faiella's daughters:
Bianca, Gisella, Emma, Elvira

While the boys were too young to even know they were in another country, Luigi's daughters felt lonely and out of place in their new home. Eugenia quietly pleaded with her husband to take her back to Prezza with her children and baby. Eugenia was a dignified lady who didn't scream and yell like most people in her family. But she felt strongly on this point, and persisted.

The women were in luck. Luigi's plan to start a new business (spices, coffee, wine, who knows?) was short-lived. After forty days in South America, the family returned to Prezza. But, the servants and their families remained in Brazil where jobs were plentiful.

Within days of their return to Prezza, Luigi went back to playing cards. The new servants did not have the same loyalty as those he had taken to Brazil. They profited by carrying away large numbers of olives while Luigi ignored his duties. Nonetheless, his fortune held out.

Luigi had visited Canada and the States several times. He made plans to move the family to North America, and decided on Chicago. But daughter Elvira refused to leave Italy without her boy friend and her mother Eugenia refused to leave Italy without her daughter. Luigi did what he had to do. His daughter was in love, so he gave the boy of eighteen a money belt that would convince immigration that he deserved to be in the United States in spite of being lame.

By the time the Faiellas moved to Chicago around the turn of the century, they had seven children, and within four years, they had two *more* boys, Aristide and Gaetano.

Emma married and had a daughter Philomena. She could never adjust to American ways and carried her sense of privilege with her. When grocery shopping, she still wore white elbow-length gloves and large hats, and rode to town in a cab.

The entire Faiella family except for Bianca and her husband moved from Chicago to the area called The Point in Quincy, Massachusetts. Emma and Philomena came to join them from their home in Pennsylvania.

The Faiella Family circa 1950 SEATED: Eugenia (L); Luigi (R);
FRONT: Giovanna; Giselda; Emma; Bianca; Elvira; BACK: Nunzio;
Arnoldo (De Nicola); Rudolpho; Amerigo; Aristide; Gaetano

THE PASQUALE FAMILY

The Pasquale family had been farmers and landowners in
Prezza. Their son Sabatino (who would one day be my grandfather)
was an educated man, having learned to speak English while in
school in the small hill town. Nonetheless, changes in Italian
economics made survival difficult for his family. Sabatino was not
of the same class as the Faiellas.

Sabatino's father Panfilo was a stern man with little empathy.
He and his wife Maria (née Forgione) had three children
together—Sabatino (my grandfather,) Micarosa, and Giojena
(pron. Joe éena.)

Great grandparents Panfilo and Maria (née) Forgione

In order to give their only son Sabatino greater economic stability, Panfilo and Maria wanted him either to marry well or to go into the priesthood. He left the seminary after witnessing the behavior of the priests, and then avoided marriage to a bride his parents had chosen for him. Sabatino fled to America in 1905 on a ship out of Naples and never saw his parents or his sister Micarosa again.

After Giojena married in Italy, she and her husband Domenico Di Bartolomeo moved to Watkins Glen, New York, and Sabatino and Giojena were able to visit now and again.

Sabatino paid a price for his freedom. He sacrificed his family, his country, and life as he'd known it.

Sabatino Pasquale and Emma Faiella had met briefly in their small mountain village in Italy and had known each other well enough to say, "Buon giorno."

They met again in the North End of Boston where many Italians lived and shopped for fresh produce and pasta. By then, Emma had married, divorced, and had a beautiful little girl named Philomena.

Emma (Grandmother) with daughter Philomena in Quincy, MA

In Boston it was unique to find someone from your own village in Italy who understood what you were saying. While Sabatino and Emma could read, speak, and understand Roman Italian, they used the local dialect of Prezza. Being able to chat comfortably while enjoying the familiar ambiance of the North End with its vegetable carts, shops, and restaurants was undoubtedly a very attractive advantage for a young couple. The familiar smells and sounds must have reminded them of the homeland they missed.

When Sabatino met Emma's daughter Philomena (Philly), he instantly loved her; it was his nature. Sabatino and Emma married in 1912, and he embraced her child as his own.

When my Aunt Philomena was in her nineties, she told me she remembered the day her mother married her new father Sabatino. It was a beautiful day at Castle Island in South Boston, and the sun glistened on her mother's lovely rose satin dress. (I found this to be curious since the Irish of South Boston were no friends to the Italians in the North End. It was all about jobs and political power and the situation didn't improve until the Irish and Italians began to marry each other in the 1940s.)

Sabatino Pasquale

CHAPTER THREE

Maternal Ancestors

THE LEET FAMILY

Elizabeth Livingston Rodger (Bessie) was born in 1900 in Glasgow, Scotland. Though I never could substantiate it, I was told that her grandmother's maiden name was Livingston and that she was part of the family of David Livingston, the famous Scottish missionary, abolitionist, and physician known for his explorations of Africa.

Bessie's life was full of challenges after her mother died in 1901 when Bessie was only a year old. Her father William Rodger, a stingy and sour man, left Scotland swiftly after his wife's death to live in Nova Scotia, Canada. Bessie lived with her maternal grandmother in Scotland until she was thirteen, when she joined her father William. By that time he was married to a woman who was mentally ill and cruel. Bessie's stepmother beat and abused her. She received no solace from her father who remained cold and distant.

Eventually William divorced Bessie's stepmother who, ultimately, was committed to a mental institution for her remaining years.

When Bessie was almost a grown woman, William married again. His third wife Mary was a loving woman who helped to ameliorate William's coldness. Mary reportedly loved Bessie, and in the end, a strong relationship of mutual respect and love developed between them.

Bessie married Geoffrey Leet in Halifax, Nova Scotia, and together they had six children, one of whom (Eva) grew up with Bessie's parents, William and Mary. The Leets lived in Braintree for most of their lives and Geoffrey worked in the shipyard.

I've written extensively of my grandfather Geoffrey's distance from my mother and me, his bigotry, and the havoc he created for my parents. But what hasn't been evident is the fact that Geoffrey had genetic connections to famous people. I found that he was a direct descendant of Geoffrey Chaucer, the father of English literature; Geoffrey was related to famous poets and writers like Emily Dickinson and Robert Frost. There were connections to Presidents, governors, movie stars (Gregory Peck and Katharine Hepburn,) and famous abolitionists like George Wythe and Louisa May Alcott.

Famous abolitionists? What in hell happened to my grandfather Geoffrey? He had decent parents (I was told) and ancestors with fabulous legacies, yet *he* left a legacy of poor choices. He kept fathering children when he couldn't take care of them. He whipped his children; he turned his back on his daughter and granddaughter—he just wasn't a nice guy—there, I said it.

It wasn't until my mother's sister, my Aunt Barbara, was elderly that she talked about the wrath she had experienced at the hands of her father. There must be something we don't know about him.

CHAPTER FOUR

The Generation Before Me

My parents have both passed, and I deeply appreciate them. I wish I had been more demonstrative in acknowledging what was so obvious to others while they were alive. The two were unique and special people. Such is the nature of offspring. Most people have regrets—this is mine.

MY FATHER PANFILIO (PAMP) PASQUALE — 1918-1980

By the time I was seventy years old my parents and many of my aunts and uncles had passed away. My father was the first to pass. We lost him suddenly in 1980 and it took the wind out of the entire family. He hadn't been an ordinary man and I had always known that he was special, but the reality of his death didn't take hold until I was ready to feel his loss.

My father was passionate, volatile, argumentative, and sometimes difficult. But he lived in the moment and everyone knew his heart was enormous and this made up for all the rest. He took risks—love often requires them—and he left a legacy of courage, generosity, humor, a love of music, and the ability to turn every day into a holiday. I see him in my children who easily and often take center stage both literally and figuratively.

Pamp at age 22

MY MOTHER DOROTHY ELIZABETH LEET — 1921- 2009

My mother's faith in Jesus gave her strength and she relied on Him and on me to keep her safe. My mother Dorothy's anxiety was palpable and I came to understand it. Her family was dirt poor when she was growing up; she had raised her siblings and never had a childhood. As a young woman she had worked in a laundry to help her family during her father's illness and was told she had a "bad" heart by a family doctor, who, I later learned, was a "quack." She kept working.

Dorothy Elizabeth Leet, 21 years old

My mother was a dignified and classy woman. When she met my father, life changed for her. When Dorothy married Pamp, it caused an upheaval in the family—the Italian Catholic drama took its toll on her. Taught that she would go to hell if she married out of her faith—in her wisdom, she knew better. Yet, her church had been the most stable part of her life.

As a young married woman, my mother struggled to make ends meet. My father's job in the shipyard with its strikes and layoffs added to her anxiety. While my father always had confidence in his ability to take care of us, my mother found it very stressful.

The multiple premature losses of her father, mother, husband, and son were each traumatic and she worried that I would somehow be next. As a result of the struggles and trauma of her past my mother lived life in a cloud of anxiety that she believed could burst at any time. This darkness obstructed my view of her and the world, and as a result I never saw her amazing wisdom and grace. While I always honored my mother and took care of her, I wish now that I had done more.

When I was a child my mother was always worried about me, and about my future. When I became an adult, things changed.

She was my mother and I was hers. It was as if I would be swallowed up if I got too close to her or she would implode if I wasn't there to rescue her.

Paul was the only one who could see how my mother unknowingly treated me and he understood the difficult position I was in. He always validated me when I most needed it, and for that I am grateful.

While my mother never asked anything of me, she didn't have to—and she appreciated everything I did for her. I gave her all I had, willingly and with love, and she did the same. But my mother and I both knew it wasn't enough.

Now I can appreciate her fully and with understanding, and in retrospect, I'm in *awe* of who she was. She always saw right and wrong clearly and she was extremely kind and understanding to all. She was never vindictive and never held a grudge. My father's care-free attitude was a torture for my mother, because she believed she had to worry for him and for all of us. I now appreciate what it was like to be her—I was she—until I found myself.

In the end she suffered. She had fought to keep going, but finally she said it was too much for her. I stayed with her until she breathed her last breath.

CHAPTER FIVE

Maternal Aunts and Uncles

THE LEET SIBLINGS

My mother Dorothy had four sisters: Peggy (Margaret), Barbara, Eva, and Mary, and one brother Geoffrey. By 2015 my mother's sister Eva and her brother Geoffrey were the only surviving relatives on her side. Aunt Eva continues to be the sweetest of the sweet and she delights the people in the nursing home every day. Uncle Geoffrey got the writer's gene—he was a sports writer for The Brockton Enterprise in Massachusetts until he retired. Geoffrey passed away in February of 2016.

The Leet Siblings c. 1985: Barbara, Eva,
Dorothy, Geoffrey, Peggy, and Mary

Aunt Peggy and Aunt Barbara were the kind of aunts that most people my age had—supportive, proud of their children and nieces and nephews, and happy to be mothers. Being wives and mothers is what they loved and what they believed they were born for. Though my mother Dorothy had to endure the challenge of marrying an Italian Catholic, it's interesting to note that Peggy and Mary married Italians as well.

All the Leet girls were pretty, but Mary was particularly beautiful. My mother and her sisters worked hard to stay young—Aunt Mary worked harder.

SEATED Pat and Peggy (Leet) Copolla at their wedding anniversary party; STANDING: *Leet* aunts and uncles: *Geoffrey*, Carole, Pamp, *Dorothy*, Eddie, *Barbara*, Larry, *Eva*, John, and *Mary*

CHAPTER SIX

Paternal Aunts – The Pasquale Women

Pasquale family photo taken at a wedding. SEATED: Egla (Cookie); Mary; Emma (Mah); Philomena (Philly); Irma (Betty): STANDING: Mario, Panfilio (Pamp); Aristide (Eddie); Sabatino (Pah); Luigi (Punky); Ulysses (Willy); and Rudolpho (Rudy)

AUNT PHILLY

Aunt Philly (Philomena) was the oldest. She and her husband Nunzio (Nudzaday) had five children: Mary, Geanette, Gloria, Dee Dee (Antoinette), and Sonny (Anthony). Sonny went ice skating one day when he was eleven and the next day he was gone—lost to pneumonia. His death broke our family's heart.

Aunt Philly knitted blankets and christening dresses and tended her garden. She loved her home and she made homemade pasta until she was nearly a hundred. Aunt Philly was a woman of high principle. She always came to the defense of the underdog, standing up for anyone who was maligned. Name-calling was something she would not tolerate.

Her children cared for her tenderly throughout her life until the end. When I visited her two days before she died, she was "with her Mah" (my grandma Emma.) She started her life alone with her mother and she left holding her hand in her mind's eye. She died at 101.

Aunt Philly and Uncle Nunzio on their wedding day

AUNT MARY

Aunt Mary and Uncle Benny Cerasoli had two children, Dolores and Bobby (Robert Angelo).

I always felt close to my Aunt Mary who lived across the street from us on Edinboro Road. She was always watching over me.

Aunt Mary had a certain dignity about her and was the least flamboyant of my father's sisters. She'd been a successful businesswoman, and in her mid-eighties, she decided to go back to work and taught two young women how to run a beauty shop. "They won't renew a license for a woman your age, Ma," my cousin Dolores said.

"What do they think—I'm 108?" my aunt replied.

Aunt Mary went back to work and lived into her nineties.

The scene at Aunt Mary's bedside before her passing was priceless: A lovely Iraqi woman dressed in a beautiful *hijab* came into Aunt Mary's room and quietly placed a large vase of flowers on the table. She sat down on the chair next to my aunt. "We miss you every day, Mary, we really miss you," she said.

"I miss you, too," my aunt said.

"We love you very much, you are part of our family." The woman lifted my aunt's hand to kiss it gently, and a tear slid down the side of her cheek.

"Where is Abuti?" my aunt asked. "I love my little Abuti, he's such a sweet little boy."

We could hear the children playing in the street as the neighbor went to the door and summoned her son. The little boy came in and stood away from her bed. His mother gently moved him closer.

"Hello, Mary," the little boy said.

"Hello, Abuti," she replied.

It was then we could all see the love Aunt Mary felt for him.

Cousin Dolores and Aunt Mary (Maria) Cerasoli, 2005

AUNT BETTY

Aunt Betty (Irma) died in 2003 at ninety after falling and hitting her head while shoveling snow. She had a notable life—she ran her own dress shop and in later years acquired a real estate license and became the number one agent in several towns located South of Boston. She said her success was due to the fact that first she told people every bad thing about the houses she was selling and then "let the chips fall where they may." If customers liked the homes in spite of their flaws, she knew she'd made an honest and happy deal. She was always pleased when she found a suitable house for "a *nice* customer."

Aunt Betty (Irma)

Aunt Betty was very bright and creative. She was defined by her energy and vibrant personality and it was really fun to be with her. Uncle Jim, her first husband, died early in their marriage and left my aunt in a position of relative wealth. Her generosity subsequently supported our extended family through many financial trials and tribulations.

Several years later, she married an Irishman named Frank Ridge—a saint who adored her and thought that everything she did was wonderful. Aunt Betty never had children, but she indulged her nieces and nephews—and delightfully, she indulged *me*.

In later years, Cousin Dolores, Aunt Cookie, and I would go with Aunt Betty to visit Uncle Frank in the *Soldiers and Sailors Home* in East Boston. Aunt Betty would spontaneously break into song—a very loud rendition of "Don't Cry For Me Argentina." As she assumed the role of Madonna in *Evita*, a group of aging war veterans would sit amused and smiling in the adjoining courtyard of the facility.

One afternoon after visiting Uncle Frank, we took the subway back home. When my aunts spotted a homeless man singing and plunking away on his guitar at the top of the escalator at the Charles Street subway station, they joined him in singing his favorite tunes.

AUNT COOKIE

Aunt Betty had an uncanny sense of how far to go with her amusing antics without making people feel uncomfortable. Aunt Cookie (Egla) was quite another matter. She was outrageous, feared nothing, and would plow ahead with no sense of social boundaries. She too had an enormous heart; but unlike her sisters, she was a person to be reckoned with.

Aunt Cookie (Egla)

She was quick to say *ma' va te ne a fanculo* (you don't want to know what it means) and cared little about what people thought of her—in her own eyes she was perfect. Her husband, Uncle Bill, was a police officer and he thought everything she did was just fine.

When my cousin Bobby ran for political office, Aunt Cookie offered to help him with his campaign. He was terrified. She insisted on working the phones and when someone refused to vote for Bobby, she swore at them and hung up. So Bobby "reassigned her" to hold up a sign on voting day outside the building. A voter approached and Aunt Cookie demanded that he vote for her nephew. The man gave her a thumbs-down. She grabbed the sign with two hands and ran after him in an attempt to hit him with it. "You bastard," she yelled. The man was dumbfounded.

Aunt Cookie had beautiful legs well into her eighties and loved to show them off. I always cringed when she started dancing around proudly. As she spun around faster and faster her dress would swirl higher and higher. We always held our breaths—but luckily the inevitable never happened.

Her son Billy had won a lawsuit and when he passed away Aunt Cookie inherited it. When she died she made a huge difference in the lives of her family. She fulfilled the promise she'd made and gave her remaining siblings and each of her nieces and nephews a gift.

CHAPTER SEVEN

Paternal Uncles – The Pasquale Men

MY FATHER'S BROTHERS

The Pasquale boys and their father FRONT: Punky, Rudy, Eddie;
SECOND ROW: Sabatino (Pah), Willie; BACK: Mario

UNCLE WILLIE (ULYSSES)

Uncle Willie and Aunt Gloria lived across the street from us on Edinboro Road with their two children Susan and Stevie (Stephen) who were younger than I. By the time they were old enough to play outside in the yard in the Point, our family had moved to Braintree. My cousin Susan, an exceptional person, was devoted to both her mother and father.

Uncle Willie was a great singer and dancer. He had learned his trade as a mason from his father. As a skilled artisan, he was always willing to donate his talents to a family member.

Willie and Eddie Pasquale

UNCLE MARIO

Uncle Mario was a veteran of the World War II. He joined the Quincy Fire Department where he worked until he retired. He and Aunt Kay had one son Joseph (Joey).

Uncle Mario was very tall and very skinny and was always eager to join in the fun. He was at every party and won the International Nose Contest. He lived into his eighties in my grandparents' house on Edwards Street.

UNCLE EDDIE (ARISTIDE)

Uncle Eddie has always been the guy that everyone wants to dance with, and though all the siblings sing, he was the *best* singer. He routinely performed at weddings and parties and I sometimes harmonized with him. He loves to use double talk and people think the problem is theirs until they realize what he's doing. And then everyone has a good laugh.

UNCLE RUDY (RUDOLPHO)

Uncle Rudy was a veteran of the Korean War and was very proud of his service. He was the youngest Pasquale child and can be seen as a young teen in pictures with Dolores and me when we were little girls in The Point. Uncle Rudy is best known as the family accordion player. Of all my uncles, I believe he was the sweetest.

After Pah died, Rudy began his work for the city of Quincy. He was a simple man who found dignity in a day's work.

He was diagnosed with stage 4 lung cancer. He never complained, he loved everyone, and he didn't worry about a thing. He was released for awhile from Hospice because he just kept on keeping on. He passed away in April of 2016.

Dickie, Sandra, Dolores, and Rudy holding
Robert Angelo (Bobby), the birthday boy

UNCLE PUNKY (LUIGI)

Luigi Pasquale (called Lou) is fondly called Uncle Punky
by our family. He is the third Pasquale son and looks the most
like his father Sabatino. He isn't a large man, but he has a huge
presence. Though not formally educated, he's very smart. He has
a finely-tuned intuition about life and people, skills that helped
him become a successful businessman in Boston.

During World War II, Uncle Punky had been presumed
missing in action. My cousin Dolores remembers the family
convening in her small living room in the Point to process what
was happening. She recalled my father crying while standing on

a chair and yelling and cursing God for taking his brother, which frightened her.

So that his mother Emma wouldn't know Luigi was missing, my father sent her letters and told her they were from her son Luigi. When my uncle was found, there was jubilation.

Uncle Punky and one other soldier had survived the bombing of an ammunition dump in Okinawa. When he was in the throes of the attack, he promised God that if he survived he would do something good for someone every day of his life—he did and he has.

My uncle greets the world with humility but he's constantly being celebrated on the radio, on television, and in the community for his contributions. Over the years he's helped countless numbers of young people, and when they grow up, they always remember what he's done for them.

Uncle Punky is a silent but effective advocate for veterans. He's relentless in his efforts to get them what they need and creatively secures resources.

In 2007, for his professional, civic, social, cultural, and charitable contributions, Uncle Punky won the "I Migliori Award" (The Best in Mind and Deed Award), a prestigious honor given to prominent people of Italian decent, previously awarded to a governor and Supreme Court Justice.

Uncle Punky still works. He's been married for upward of sixty years to Aunt Terry who is his biggest fan. They have two children—Donald and Dianne.

Uncle Punky is well-loved and revered, and will be celebrating his 90th birthday this year.

He reflects everything about my ancestry that I cherish—generosity of spirit, creative thinking, wisdom, humor, and the blind acceptance that connects him instantly to the world around him. All of who he is has been woven through my past like threads of many colors. How very fortunate I am to have had him for all these years in the absence of my father, his father, and all the others who came before us.

Uncle Punky as a young Army PFC

CPSIA information can be obtained
at www.ICGtesting.com
Printed in the USA
BVOW04s1808261116

468969BV00003B/190/P